Praise for

"Patricia writes with the lived experience of having worked with some of the best, and some of the worst, senior executives on the matter of diversity, in all the forms it takes. As a leading executive recruiter working on the most challenging board and executive roles, Patricia has unique insight into why diversity is still a problem today after all this time talking about what can be done about it. She has a wealth of data to add to the equation and is a leading proponent of getting enough people of diverse backgrounds a seat at the main table to ensure their talent is captured and the business benefits associated from doing this are realized."

—Elizabeth Aris, *group executive, entrepreneur, non-executive director*

"Patricia brings the right combination of empathy, awareness, and focus to drive corporate profitability through diversity of thought and people. She is one of the most talented and emotionally intelligent people I know to help corporations lead with purpose and profit."

—Dee M. Robinson, *CEO, Robinson Hill; growth/scaling strategist; gaming industry expert, DE&I advocate; board member*

"Patricia's direct but thoughtful approach models the strategies she herself advocates. *Time's Up: Why Boards Need to Get Diverse Now* is a wake-up call and a toolkit to anyone who influences the composition of a board. Underrepresented communities need allies like Patricia to continue to advocate for what is a complete no-brainer—gender, racial, ethnic, and sexual orientation diversity on a board is good for business. Leaders who read this book will walk away with a list of actionable items including smart recruiting strategies to identify and connect with diverse leaders."

—Ozzie Gromada Meza, *Head of Membership and Talent Intelligence, Latino Corporate Directors Association*

"*Time's Up: Why Boards Need to Get Diverse Now* translates a tremendously important subject into a comprehensive, easy-to-read guide for directors. Patricia Lenkov shares important research on board diversity and offers an illuminating road map for how to broaden the perspectives in your boardroom. Boards are accountable for successful companies, and diverse viewpoints ensure robust debate—a key component of effectively overseeing management and constructively challenging company performance and its execution of strategy. As Patricia says, 'Let's get going. Let's move forward.' *Time's Up* is a must-read for all directors."

—Denise Kuprionis, *President, The Governance Solutions Group*

"Patricia Lenkov's timely and compelling *Time's Up* reminds us that if America is enriched by her diverse cultural mosaic then we should expect no less for corporate boards. A widely recognized talent expert and diversity champion, Lenkov offers boards a road map for how they can widen their apertures, draw from the nation's abundant and untapped talent, and be optimized assets propelling their companies to greater achievement."

—Michael Montelongo, *19th Assistant Secretary of the Air Force for Financial Management & Comptroller; and independent board director*

PATRICIA LENKOV

TIME'S UP

WHY
BOARDS
NEED TO
GET DIVERSE
NOW

Printed in the United States of America.
Library of Congress Control Number: 2021911887
ISBN: 978-1-73511-128-5

Cover Design: David Taylor
Layout Design: Wesley Strickland

To Gabriella, Ethan and Brandon who show me every day why diverse ideas and original thinking can change the world.

And to Robert who has supported me on every step of this journey. Thank you for never giving up on me and this project.

CONTENTS

INTRODUCTION

Together we can do great things.

—MOTHER THERESA

If you are a corporate executive, investor, employee, or other stake-holder of a company, I need to share a little secret with you: your board of directors may be suboptimal and, as such, undermining your growth and profitability.

I know what you are thinking. All types of factors are responsible for a decrease in corporate growth and profitability, including

- COVID-19 and the fallout of the pandemic,

- the impact of Amazon on the distribution and pricing of goods, from automobiles to zippers,

- the lingering effects of the financial crisis of 2008,

- the alleged lack of qualified workers in manufacturing and high tech, and

- the emergence of competitive economies around the world, from Argentina to the United Arab Emirates.

Nobody worth their salt would downplay the importance of any one of these issues. In fact, you would want your board members to take each of them—and dozens of other factors—into account

Current research stretching back nearly twenty years tells us that one of the contributors to disappointing company results is the composition of the board of directors.

when contemplating your company's business goals: increasing revenue, designing new products and services, entering new markets, and becoming the top-of-mind brand, to name a few. But is your board of directors capable of doing this?

What if your board members are so similar in age, educational background, and corporate experience that they are consistently of one mind (or similar minds) on every issue the company faces? Is uniformity and consensus what a corporate board really needs?

Current research stretching back nearly twenty years tells us that one of the contributors to disappointing company results is the composition of the board of directors. Not only C-level executives. Not only middle management. Not only HR. Not only employees. These individuals may be talented and even brilliant, but they are not the only ones responsible for the strategic direction your company decides to take. That task is overseen, contributed to, and signed off on by the board of directors.

As such, your board composition must be carefully configured so that it is optimized for the best possible results. And it must be adjusted (perhaps even reconfigured) at regular intervals to keep up with the natural changes any company faces.

Indeed, management researchers at Portland State University and North Carolina State University published a study in late 2017 linking diverse corporate boards and future innovative efficiency.[1] Research published in the *Journal of Economic Research* in May 2018 found that "diversity contributes value by providing access to a greater volume of information or skills by incorporating the best board members regardless of gender, age or nationality."[2]

Corporate homogeneity hasn't escaped the notice of investment management firms either. The largest institutional investors in the world—BlackRock, State Street, and Vanguard—have all proclaimed diversity to be a high priority and have acted to effect change. In 2017, CtW Investment Group, a Washington, DC–based pension fund investment firm, blamed the lack of growth and poor stock performance at Urban Outfitters on a board dominated by what one reporter called "oldish white dudes."[3] "For a company that is so reliant on global sourcing and focused on women, it is surprising that the board consists of largely Caucasian males with law and finance backgrounds," CtW stated.

To be fair, the Philadelphia-based clothier now has three women on its board, although one is the chief executive's wife. It's progress of the mincing sort, but it's a start. It should be noted that more recently Anthropologie, a division of Urban Outfitters, was accused of the use of racial profiling to target Black potential shoplifters in their stores. The board of directors does not have any Black directors at the time of writing.

A 2014 biannual report by the Credit Suisse Research Institute found that gender diversity in senior management was linked to "excess stock market returns and superior corporate profitability."[4] And the 2016 Global Board Diversity Analysis performed by executive search firm Egon Zehnder said right off the bat that for gender diversity to make a meaningful impact, a board must have three women directors.[5]

As you'll see in the coming chapters, research that draws either a causal connection or a correlation between corporate success and board diversity is abundant and convincing. Increasingly, corporations are acting on that research, not always because they are moved by a sense of social fairness but because more diverse boards make solid business sense. We cannot know for sure what effect female leadership representation would have had on the Weinstein Company or the *New York Times*, two companies rocked in 2017 by confirmed reports of sexual harassment. At the very least, the presence of women would reflect an "environment where women are viewed as leaders, peers, and colleagues, and not prey," as corporate board advisor Brande Stellings has said.[6]

An unintended consequence of the #MeToo movement—a social-media campaign to expose the reality of sexual assault and harassment in the workplace—is that companies of all sizes can no longer be cavalier about the absence of women on their boards. Gone are the days when board members could tell me that "we have better things to worry about," as one did in 2013 shortly after California passed Resolution 62 to "encourage equitable and diverse gender representation on corporate boards."[7] Resolution 62 was the precursor to the legal quota that now exists in California for more gender diversity on boards. Resolution 62 urged corporations to have more gender diversity; the new quota requires the change.

Similarly, the fallout of the tragic murder of George Floyd in 2020 provided the much-needed catalyst for new discussions about the lack of Black people on boards and in leadership positions in corporate America.

Change is slow—too slow—but more and more common are initiatives by organizations such as investment firm BlackRock, which has said that companies need to contribute to society if they want to continue receiving investment support.[8]

As the overseer of $7.4 trillion in investments, BlackRock founder and chief executive Larry D. Fink intends to put his money where his mouth is. Fink cites board diversity in a list of socially important issues that includes immigration policy, race relations, gay rights, children's health, and climate change. The task of overseeing "environmental, social, and governance" matters[9] in all investment strategies is assigned to Michelle Edkins, global head of investment stewardship, who oversees a team of thirty focused on these matters.

In case companies don't quite get what "fostering more effective engagement" means, Fink spells it out: "Boards with a diverse mix of genders, ethnicities, career experiences, and ways of thinking … are less likely to succumb to groupthink or miss new threats to a company's business model. And they are better able to identify opportunities that promote long-term growth."[10]

Money talks in a way that my own rational pleading as a corporate board matchmaker often did not.

I saw what I was up against when I first got into the business of executive search. I joined Heidrick & Struggles, a worldwide executive search firm, in 1997. I came in with about ten years' experience in various industry and university roles, but in senior-level search and board recruiting, I was wet behind the ears. I was incredibly lucky to report to a woman, a former IBM executive, who got me involved in all her CEO and board searches, and whose own business acumen eventually landed her a job in President George W. Bush's administration as assistant for presidential personnel. In short, I learned executive search from the best of the best and got to meet some of the world's most impressive corporate leaders from the get-go.

Early on I accompanied my boss to my first public company board meeting. We were doing a CEO search for a publicly traded technology company headquartered in the western United States. Being somewhat introverted by nature, I admit I was intimidated at the prospect of meeting the board's movers and shakers. I pictured a room full of high-octane visionaries, brilliant men and women who had helped oversee and guide this high-growth and preeminent software business. A huge success story in what was then the nascent technology industry. Who was I to even breathe the same air they did?

Was I ever in for an eye-opener.

When I entered the boardroom, I saw a bunch of elderly White men dressed in cardigans shuffling around the long oval table. Cardigans! Like this was a senior center and they had all gotten together for the early-bird special. And at the beginning of the board meeting, what were they most interested in? They just had to know if they were going to have that amazing food from the local Chinese restaurant for lunch.

I wish I could say nothing like that board meeting ever happened again. But I can recall many a meeting with board directors or a subset of their members where my presence was met with confusion and bewilderment. Was I there to contribute or take dictation and serve coffee?

We're talking about 1998 here, not 1950.

Time's up.

Time's up for corporate board members who hide behind personal biases that are hobbling companies and keeping them from becoming truly great.

Time's up for companies that pay lip service to all the "fearless girls" they hire and then pay less than their male counterparts.

Time's up for companies that pay Black executives less than their White colleagues.

Time's up for board members who don't intimately understand their client base's tastes, preferences, and shopping habits.

Time's up for senior executives and board members who shunt women into the role of chief marketing officer or chief human resources officer.

Time's up for the sheep on corporate boards.

Time's up, too, for making uninformed business decisions that result in rejecting a young but paradigm-shifting start-up (Excite passed on buying Google), designing a product nobody wants (as Coca-Cola did in 1985), and quashing homegrown

A diverse board is not a talisman against every corporate miscalculation, but neither is the male, pale, and stale boardroom a path to the next big thing.

technology because it threatens the profitability of current products (Kodak sat on digital camera and cell phone technology in favor of its disposable camera business).[11] How many better decisions could have been made if these companies' corporate boards had consisted of a thirty-year-old Bill Gates (Microsoft), a thirty-five-year-old Ellen Ochoa (Johnson Space Center), a forty-year-old Vera Wang (Vera Wang Group), a forty-five-year-old Robin Chase (Zipcar), or a twenty-seven-year-old Neil deGrasse Tyson (Hayden Planetarium)?

A diverse board is not a talisman against every corporate miscalculation, but neither is the male, pale, and stale boardroom a path to the next big thing. As a member of a business community whose decisions ultimately affect every woman, man, and child on this planet, I want to share with corporations everywhere the business case for diverse corporate boards and the path to achieving this long overdue fundamental.

The business case—not a do-the-right-thing lecture that might guilt-trip you into adding a token woman, person of color, or representative of the LGBTQ+ community to your board. You need to make choices based on your need to become more profitable and grow as a company.

Frankly, I am not a takin'-it-to-the-streets person. Don't look for me marching through my Manhattan neighborhood with pink headgear, because I won't be there. While it is an effective strategy for many, where you will find me is where I have been for the past twenty-four years: in corporate boardrooms in Canada, the United States, Israel, and elsewhere. The more than three hundred and fifty board searches I have done have acquainted me intimately with the mindset of the most influential business leaders in high tech, consumer products, retail, and finance—basically almost every industry. I can vouch that every single one of them has had the best interests of their companies at heart. Admittedly, some were fossils who were suspicious of anybody who had not gone to the same schools they'd attended or who had not worked for the same handful of companies. And some had never really gotten out of the who-do-we-know rut that results in—I hate to say it—a board full of clones.

And incidentally, the conversation about diversity in boardrooms and senior leadership teams is still rather simplistic. We speak of two genders and four or five types of ethnicity, and we are just beginning to consider the LGBTQ+ community as worthy of mention within the realm of leadership and boardrooms. In the not-too-distant future, for a variety of social and economic reasons, we may also be asked to pay attention to age, social class, and disability when constructing boards and executive teams.

I wrote *Time's Up: Why Boards Need to Get Diverse Now* to help companies do the right thing—for their bottom line, for their product development, and for a future that is changing before our eyes. A diverse board will help you get ready for an economy where consumers share rather than own, where employees work as often from their living rooms as from an open office space, and where C-suite executives need to understand a complex, diverse, unpredictable marketplace.

Let's get going. Let's move forward.

There's still time.

CHAPTER 1

EXECUTIVE SEARCH IS PART OF THE PROBLEM

It is the mark of an educated mind that a person can entertain a thought without having to accept it.

—ARISTOTLE

t is tempting to put all the blame on global corporations for the absence of women and ethnic minorities from so many boardrooms.

Not that there isn't room for blame.

As of October 2019, women held a little more than 20 percent of all corporate board seats in the Russell 3000.[12] In terms of non-White ethnic minorities, they currently hold 10 percent of board seats in the Russell 3000. Just as a matter of reference, according to US census, this demographic represents 24 percent of the US population. For minority women on the Fortune 500, that figure drops to an alarming 3 percent.[13]

What is to blame for these numbers? The usual suspects:

- human nature

- rigid definition about what qualifies one to be a board member

- gender, racial, and ethnic discrimination

- laziness and unconscious bias

- belief that qualified candidates do not exist

The fact is that when board seats become available, they often go to people much like the people already on the board: White male CEOs and former CEOs.

Like birthday parties and high school gym teams, board selection operates on what behavioral researchers call the "representativeness heuristic." In plain English, that means, "like goes to like." Just look around at your closest friends. Chances are you went to similar schools and raised your kids in the same neighborhoods. You may root for the same sports team and think alike politically. You might even share the same religion or race. Interacting with people most like ourselves helps us make many judgments with accuracy and ease.[14] It helps us simplify a very complex world. But it can also limit our peripheral vision about matters outside our own immediate experience—including decisions about the value of diversity.

It is common knowledge in governance circles that about 70 percent of the time, finding a new board director goes like this: The current board, CEO, and trusted advisors talk among themselves about the people they know who could fill an empty board seat. One of the main attributes for recruitment? The candidate is already part of the corporate world's inner sanctum. Board members already know him or know people who know him. Why not choose somebody familiar and connected in some way? Better safe than sorry.

This search process may feel safe, but the results are often sorry.[15]

Regrettably, executive search firms, the go-to choice in about 30 percent of board search scenarios, have been part of the problem too. Here's how a board search typically goes when an executive search firm is hired: The CEO or, hopefully, the chair of the board's nominating and governance committee gets in touch with his long-term recruiter, a fellow much like himself in terms of family background, education, and social standing. If he is "of a certain age," the recruiter might flip through his trusty Rolodex or browse his ever-ready and rarely evolving "board list." If he is more tech savvy, he accesses his "proprietary" database and compiles a list of potential board directors. And guess what? They will generally be known. Perhaps a former client or board placement. The same demographic as the CEO, the committee chair, and the recruiter. In this way, this search process is restricted, exclusive, and uncreative. The frequent result: a pool of candidates who are well known, predictable, and conventional.

To further illustrate this circuitous system, look at the leadership of three of the largest executive search firms, whose names I have anonymized out of respect for friends and colleagues who work at them:

- Firm A: The global leadership team consists of sixteen people. Six are women. The only one who is non-Caucasian heads the Asia-Pacific business.

- Firm B: Has a board practice with several leaders. None are people of color and one was referred to as "fossilized" in a 2004 article in *Fortune* magazine.

- Firm C: Has a board search practice with thirty-five consultants in the US. Of these, one is a person of color.

Not overly egregious. However, as advocates of diversity, should they not have more diversity in their corner offices and boardrooms? Also, these are three of the largest and most well-established firms in the world and as such will be further evolved than the thousands of midsize and small firms.

These firms are not completely tone-deaf. They have recently begun to hear the outcry against the underrepresentation of women and minorities in decision-making roles in virtually every industry. And for that we can thank, in large part, institutional investors, grass-roots efforts to organize and to improve diversity—such as Catalyst and the Executive Leadership Council (ELC), as well as the Latino Corporate Directors Association—and those corporate leaders who do have the determination to push the boundaries on these issues. The #MeToo movement and protests against racism have undoubtedly also played a role.

Indeed, no company can afford to ignore the inclusion and diversity issues that increasingly link women, Black people, Hispanics, Asians, and the LGBTQ+ community to the health of a company's bottom line.

Boards without women show an average return on equity of 11 percent, compared with 16.7 percent for boards with three or more women.

The research underpinning this premise stretches back at least to 2007 when Catalyst, a global nonprofit helping organizations accelerate progress for women at work, published a report that suggested "alignment" between the presence of women in boardrooms and strong performance at Fortune 500 companies. Among the areas in which the presence of women has a favorable impact on a company's bottom line are:

- *Return on equity.* Companies with more women board directors (WBD) outperform those with the least women by 53 percent.

- *Return on sales.* Companies with the most WBD outperform those with the least by 42 percent.

- *Return on invested capital.* Companies with more WBD outperform those with the least by 66 percent.

Catalyst also found that stronger-than-average results prevail at companies where at least three women serve on a board. For example, boards without women show an average return on equity of 11 percent, compared with 16.7 percent for boards with three or more women. This is important to note because so often companies believe that they are done once they appoint that single female or ethnic minority to their board. We have an expression to describe this phenomenon: "one and done." But there is in fact a tipping point only after which real change and improvement can occur.

In fact, Catalyst found the link between women board directors and corporate performance to be true even across varied industries. This was especially relevant for organizations in consumer goods, healthcare, industrials, and information technology.[16]

Two years later, management researchers at the University of Oklahoma and the University of Wisconsin (Madison) also found that many firms, "from Bank of America to Sara Lee ... assert that board diversity leads to higher firm performance." Building on older studies about the so-called behavioral theory of the firm, the researchers wrote that "diverse human capital on boards influences the strategic direction of the firm by providing cognitive conflict which may result in innovative ideas."

In short, hashing out opposing ideas might be onerous, but it is ultimately good for business.

The same researchers also cited studies on signaling theory, the notion that companies with diverse boards fare better financially because the diversity itself signals "social laws and values" that elevate the company's reputation in the eyes of customers, consumers, suppliers, employees, and other stakeholders.[17]

With all this research available, why have executive search firms persisted in assembling male, pale, and stale boards? At the very least they should be challenging this situation and should be harbingers of best practices. They must counsel their clients on the facts and benefits of diversity at all levels of the organization and be prepared to do the hard work of looking for the not-obvious but no-less-qualified candidates.

Make no mistake, the executive recruiting industry is still filled with those who demonstrate the legacy thinking that got them to the top of their field but may no longer be enough. For instance, the business community got a look at the way one executive search consultant dealt firsthand with diversity issues in 2004 when a female colleague alleged that he fired her after their affair fizzled. The woman had coauthored an executive management book with him and run an exclusive and profitable CEO club for the firm. Yet even the accolades she received from CEOs at Fortune 100 companies did not prevent her former lover from terminating her contract. She sued him for gender discrimination. And his ex-wife vouched for her!

Quoting another male consultant at the firm, a *Fortune* magazine article in 2004 said, "It's going to hurt him within the firm."

It hasn't. Today that same male search consultant has moved on to another high-profile executive search firm where he is vice chairman of board recruitment, advising the largest companies in the land.

I knew him. He was one of the original #MeToo culprits. And his reputation at this large white-shoe search firm preceded him. Working with him was like working with an improvised explosive device that threatened to go off if you so much as smiled at him. This is a man who has placed prominent chief executives and corporate directors at many of the largest and most esteemed corporations in the world. He has been advising on leadership when he has a well-known reputation for running around the office chasing women. Everyone knew. Nobody spoke up.

Somehow ten years ago this was acceptable. A known sexual harasser could continue because he was a rainmaker. However, the flaw in this logic is that if one cannot behave morally and ethically, where is the moral compass by which to judge and evaluate others?

* * *

Let me attempt to justify my silence.

Here I was at an executive search firm, advising some of the smartest businesspeople in the world about diversity, leadership, and equitable hiring, but I wasn't practicing what I preached. I wanted to, but I was silent. The reason? Those who ran the firms and created the rules were of a certain mindset, and it was in an era when underlings did not question the status quo for fear of being labeled insubordinate.

Executive search has contributed to the lack of diversity problem for a long time. Not only in terms of the service to clients but also within their own organizations. Those hired to advise on board composition must truly, authentically, and intrinsically appreciate the value of diversity. They must be diverse. They must be more than the same old demographic.

Frankly, the people who really get shortchanged are the Fortune 500 companies that pay for executive search services and believe they are getting their money's worth. If corporations truly desire diversity, they will not accept the well-established excuse that it is a supply problem. That is "we tried, but there are simply no qualified candidates who are diverse." Companies need to know that they have been shortchanged by their trusted advisors. Unfortunately, they have been lulled into complicity, and as a result they get board members who look no different from them. Board members who do not challenge their ideas. Board members more interested in the lunch menu than in who is eating their companies' lunch!

It is bad enough that I kept my mouth shut all those years. But what about the many esteemed business news outlets? Why aren't they writing about lack of diversity among candidates supplied by executive search firms? No matter the corporate fiasco, even those where an executive lied on his or her résumé and no one caught this, the search firms are never mentioned. This is disheartening.

Let us look to the recent past to get a sense of how board searches traditionally played out. Leaders of the various search firms used to compile and maintain lists. Lists of acceptable and permittable board candidates. These invaluable lists consisted of names, titles, and companies—and not much else. When a company hired an executive search firm, these lists were the first source of prospects. In many cases they were the only source. The recruiter leading the search would scan the list and select names he or she believed to be a good match. *Believed* is the operative word here. Scientific, systematic, diagnostic, not really. Familiarity was key. This seemingly risk-mitigated approach relied on acquaintanceship as a key qualifier.

Only a handful of corporate executives ever expressed horror at this "methodology." The late Ralph Whitworth was one of them. A protégé of hedge fund manager and corporate raider T. Boone Pickens, Whitworth founded an activist investment fund in California called Relational Investors. While on the board of Hewlett-Packard and Home Depot, he solicited an executive search firm to help find a new board member for each of those companies. His jaw dropped when the firm came back to him with almost the exact same slate of candidates for both companies.

Think about it. Hewlett-Packard is a technology company. Home Depot is a retailer. Very different businesses, strategies, challenges, and the like. Yet the search firm's idea of hard work was to come up with the exact same board recommendations for two very different companies?

No wonder Whitworth became vocal about the staid composition of boards, calling them out for not "evolving with the times."[18]

Whitworth was ahead of his time when back in 2012 he stated on *This Week in the Boardroom*, a video program for board members, that "C-suite executives, and board members should be asking, 'Do we have the right devil's advocate at the table?'" He also commented, "We need to make sure the (board directors) are acting independently."

I want to believe that Ralph Whitworth's board activism touched corporate boards deep in their sleepy souls—and that those boring search lists are not being circulated anymore. But I still regularly hear from executives and board directors that they do not like to use the big search firms to recruit board members.

"They recycle the same names over and over again," many have said. They do.

But what good does it do if we in executive search know that they do—and we do not say anything about it?

Executive search must stop being part of the problem. Search firms must stop using a closed-loop system and reach out to diverse, previously untapped executives.

People like Ralph Whitworth and social movements like #MeToo have helped us see how desperate we are for a new model of corporate board recruitment. They have helped institutional investors see, too, that overcoming the tried and no-longer-true approach to composing corporate boards will take more than blaming global corporations for living in the 1950s.

"We have met the enemy and he is us!" as the cartoonist Walt Kelly said.[19]

Taking personal responsibility for our own failures is a first step. But it won't be the last.

CHAPTER 2

A BOARD WITHOUT WOMEN IS ASKING FOR TROUBLE

Never doubt that a small group of thoughtful,
committed citizens can change the world.
Indeed, it is the only thing that ever has.

—MARGARET MEAD

G ood morning, America. It is 2021, and the percentage of women on Russell 3000 boards is still a mere 20.2 percent. This number was 16.9 percent in 2018, so at least we are moving in the right direction. As of November 2019, though, 311 companies in this index still had zero women on their boards.[20]

How can this be? Women hold 60 percent of the country's personal wealth and 51 percent of all US stocks.[21] In 2017, women made up about 56 percent of students on college campuses. No matter their ethnic and racial group, by age thirty-one women are more likely than men to have received a college degree.[22] Furthermore, women are far and away the major buyers of snacks, aluminum foil, healthcare, groceries, apparel, and shoes for themselves and their families. Additionally, 50 percent of products typically marketed to men are purchased by women.[23] However, they are quite underrepresented on boards at companies such as Hostess (25 percent female board directors), Sketchers, (10 percent), Dillard's (8 percent), and Discovery, Inc. (8 percent), to name a few. Incidentally, the website of the last company on this list, Discovery, Inc., states that it has "approximately 20 percent share of women watching primetime in the US."[24] Their audience is women, so wouldn't they want women to weigh in at the highest level of the organization?

Outside the US, there are varied levels of progress on gender diversity in the boardroom. Norway leads the pack with 41 percent women on their boards. France has 37 percent, while Belgium has 30 percent. At the other end of the spectrum is Asia where women represent 9.3 percent of board seats.[25]

In this age of artificial intelligence, civilian space travel, and unprecedented personal choice, how is it that this most basic of corporate structures is still so dominated by one gender?

The answer is complex and multifaceted, and we will discuss it throughout this book. For now, let's be overly simplistic and state that there is still some legacy belief that board service is indefinite. Of course, this lack of turnover means lack of openings for new directors. It may interest some to note that among US public companies there are currently 341 directors with tenures of over thirty years and 737 with tenures of twenty years or more. The second most common reason for the lack of heterogeneity in the boardroom is the legacy belief that board directors must be CEOs.

Sure, every board could use a CEO or two, but a boardroom full of them is simply another method of exclusion.

Boards have found other ingenious ways to limit the number of women in the room. They complain about a lack of qualified women, and they recycle the few whose skills have already been tested on other boards.

The social networking service Twitter, for example, went public in 2006 with no women on its board. What followed was an outcry on traditional and social media, and everyone, from the *New York Times* to TechCrunch, was saying, "How could they do this?" Twitter's strongest criticism came from Vivek Wadhwa, a fellow at Stanford's Rock Center for Corporate Governance, who accused the "Twitter mafia" of "elite arrogance" and "male chauvinistic thinking."[26]

How did Twitter respond? We are a technology company. We are technical. We need engineers. We cannot find any women who fit the bill.

Dick Costolo, who was CEO at the time, became defensive, calling Wadhwa the "Carrot Top of academic sources."[27]

In response, article upon article offered up dozens of women with backgrounds in technology and engineering. *New York Times* reporter Claire Cain Miller helpfully produced a list of twenty-five candidates; Matthew Lynley of BuzzFeed came up with ten.[28] Finally, in 2013, Twitter appointed Marjorie Scardino to its board. At the time, Scardino was CEO of Pearson plc, a multinational publishing and education company. A nonexecutive director of Nokia and former CEO of the Economist Group, Scardino was credited with tripling Pearson's profits to a record £942 million.[29] Today, Twitter has three women on their board (27 percent gender diversity), who in addition to gender diversity, bring ethnic and geographic diversity, as well as diversity of experience. Progress.

Thanks, in part, to their well-known "Bro culture," Silicon Valley innovators have been less than innovative when it comes to boardroom gender diversity. It would not hurt these billion-dollar entrants into the business universe if they took a page from, say, Walmart's[30] playbook on boardroom diversity and seated at least three women on their boards. Or McDonald's[31] playbook. Or CVS's.[32] These companies embrace boardroom gender diversity because they have learned that healthy debate is the wellspring of creative thinking. BlackRock CEO Larry Fink agrees and believes further that corporate boards must look like the shareholders who invest in their companies and like the customers who buy their products and services.

* * *

Why is a board without women asking for trouble? To answer this question, let us look more closely at Larry Fink's recent exhortation to CEOs that they take corporate social responsibility seriously. In his 2018 letter to CEOs, Fink argues for a new business paradigm that emphasizes social consciousness as much as high performance. Because shareholders and clients are the "true owners"[33] of a company, corporate responsibility "goes beyond casting proxy votes at annual meetings." Genuine responsibility means "investing the time and resources necessary to foster long-term value."

Why is Fink so focused on the link between a company's business performance and its potential impact on society?

Fink understands that an "engaged board"—a board willing to consider ideas from a "diverse mix of genders, ethnicities, career experiences, and ways of thinking"— indicates a company's "ability to identify opportunities that promote long-term growth."

A board without women is asking for trouble because it is misaligned with the reality of the marketplace.

There it is: a correlation between board diversity and long-term growth.

Gone are the days when business issues sat on one side of an economic divide and social issues on the other. In the current environment, Fink says, all kinds of stakeholders are looking to companies to find solutions for the environmental, social, and governance issues that have bedeviled one US administration after another. Fink believes that a company's willingness to take on the big social issues of the day reflects its ability to assume "the leadership ... that is so essential to sustainable growth."

Fink suggests that government has stopped asking the big questions. Increasingly, we see that business leaders, not politicians, are the people talking about moon shots. Federal initiatives seem to have gone as far as they can in promoting workplace and educational diversity, and now it is industry's turn to debate how effectively we as a society are providing opportunity for historically underrepresented communities.

A board without women is asking for trouble because it is misaligned with the reality of the marketplace. According to Catalyst: In 2018, women were estimated to control about $40 trillion in consumer spending across the world.[34] As previously mentioned, women control most of the purchasing decisions for themselves, as well as their families. Obtaining their input and insights on business strategy is essential, and it starts in the boardroom.

Furthermore, some accounting researchers have asserted that boardroom gender diversity is an effective mechanism for alleviating real activities manipulation[35]—management actions that deviate from normal business practices, undertaken with the primary objective of meeting certain earnings thresholds[36] in the short term.

"Using a large sample of 11,831 firm-year observations [number of firms x number of years] from Chinese A-share listed firms for the 2000–2011 period, we find that when a firm has a critical mass of women serving on its [Board of Directors], i.e., at least 3 women or a high ratio of women on its board, its managers engage in less real activities manipulation," according to accounting researchers at Sun Yat-sen University in Guangdong, China. "In addition, we find that the negative relation is more pronounced when female directors hold higher ownership, indicating that stock ownership may enhance the role of female directors in curbing real activities manipulation."[37]

MSCI, a US provider of financial indexes, claims that a board without women breeds scandal. It reported in 2015 that "public companies with more women on their boards are less likely to be hit by scandals such as bribery, fraud, or shareholder battles."[38] MSCI data indicated that twelve global companies, including Bank of New York Mellon, Credit Agricole, Nokia, and Tata Motors, which had fewer women on their boards than the country average, had greater than average governance controversies over a three-year period (2011–2014).[39] In fact, I have often heard the tongue-in-cheek comment going something like, "if Lehman Brothers had been Lehman sisters, maybe they would still be around." It is well documented that women are more risk averse than men.[40]

As we continue to rightly focus on ESG issues, it is also important to note that "companies with more than average number of female directors score more highly on MSCI's metric for management of environmental, social and governance risks."[41]

Patrice Merrin, the first female director on the board of Canada-based Glencore International, a global commodities trader, asks that companies think about avoiding scandal and fostering long-term value in this way:

"I constantly ask corporate executives to keep front and center the image of their favorite schoolteacher, now eighty-five years old and in need of a home-care aide to help with the tasks of everyday life," Merrin says. "You were once a little kid in the classroom of the woman who is trusting you to steward her lifetime investments so she can live out her old age in a dignified state."[42]

"I have never known a man to put a face to what I call the 'virtuous circle of capital,'" Merrin says. "We're not talking complicated finance here. We are talking old-fashioned civic decency: Fair play. Leadership by example. I'll pass the ball to you, and you can try for a three-pointer."

Boards are being asked to weigh in on social issues and human capital in ways that are unprecedented.

* * *

To be clear, I am not asking whether women are better equipped ethically or morally to confront social issues. That proposition is far beyond the scope of this book. What I am saying, as Australian workplace equality researcher Linda Peach did, is that "diverse groups of people bring a greater variety of experience and different views to the decision-making process and then make better decisions," and that "gender diversity on boards helps to ensure that the entire consumer base is represented."[43]

A veritable tsunami of complex issues—social and governance—are rushing into the corporate boardroom. Boards are being asked to weigh in on social issues and human capital in ways that are unprecedented. It stands to reason that a diverse board will be better equipped to deal with these matters.

For example, in January 2018 JANA Partners and the California State Teachers' Retirement System (CalSTRS)—which own a total of $2 billion in Apple stock[44] and had previously collaborated on concerns of mutual interest—partnered to send a joint letter to Apple,

Inc., asking the technology company to "help ensure that young consumers are using your products in an optimal manner."[45]

Is it JANA's or CalSTRS's business how your kids are using an electronic device that you bought for them? Apparently, Barry Rosenstein, founder and managing partner at JANA, and Anne Sheehan, then head of corporate governance at CalSTRS, think it is. They teamed up with Michael Rich, founding director of the Center on Media and Child Health at Boston Children's Hospital; Jean M. Twenge, author of the book *iGen*; and musician Sting and his wife, producer Trudie Styler, to cite research that examines the impact that technology such as Apple's iPhone has on kids. Among their findings:

- US teens who spend five hours or more a day on electronic devices have a 71 percent greater suicide risk than those who spend less than one hour.

- Kids who overuse technology get less sleep.

- American parents say that regulating their child's screen time is a "constant battle."[46]

Rosenstein and those he teamed up with have asked Apple to consider developing software that would provide parents with more options to limit children's phone use.

Apple could have said, "If you don't like our product, you don't have to buy it." Company executives did not, because they are not cavalier enough to commit brand suicide. In fact, one of the inventors of the first iPhone responded by calling for Silicon Valley to start battling device addiction.

"Apple Watches, Google Phones, Facebook, Twitter—they've gotten so good at getting us to go for another click, another dopamine hit," tweeted angel investor and Nest founder Tony Fadell. "They now have a responsibility & need to start helping us track & manage our digital addictions across all usages—phone, laptop, TV etc."

The company has announced that it is developing new features to make parental controls "more robust."[47]

Would Apple have considered working on new features that make its products less addictive if grassroots pressure—much of it coming from women—had not been brought to bear?

On the surface, it looks as if JANA, a hedge fund activist, and CalSTRS, a public sector retirement fund, are advocating for greater social responsibility on the part of corporations. I would argue, as I will throughout this book, that while the push for social change and for "doing the right thing" may be a result of greater boardroom diversity, the more compelling link is between boardroom diversity and profitability. In short, pressure from investors convinced Apple that making its products less addictive would ultimately result in greater marketplace approval, which ultimately leads to improved sales and hopefully profits. It is what Patrice Merrin means when she talks about the "virtuous circle of capital."

"The truth is that the worlds of activism and impact investing are converging much more swiftly than most people realize—and this union holds enormous promise for those who wish to see the creation of capital markets that support sustainable economic development,"[48] writes Robert G. Eccles, formerly a professor of management practice at Harvard Business School and a cosignatory to the JANA-CalSTRS letter. He believes JANA is urging Apple to mitigate overuse of the iPhone because doing so will "create value for its shareholders in the long term. It's as simple as that."[49]

The discussion of activism and activist investors doing the right thing as illustrated above is not complete and accurate without also looking at the other end of the spectrum. Carl Icahn is a legendary activist investor. Eighty-five years old and experienced on such boards as Trans World Airlines, Imclone Systems (pharmaceuticals and biotechnology), and Blockbuster (retail and entertainment). Despite this, Icahn Enterprises did not have a single woman on their board until September 2019. As of 2016 his firm had nominated forty-two people to fill ninety-four board seats, and not one was female.[50]

* * *

If BlackRock, JANA Partners, Apple, and the California State Teachers' Retirement System have made the connection between gender diversity and corporate profitability, why haven't hundreds of other corporations in the US and around the world? And if BlackRock's Fink recognizes that board diversity supports social responsibility, what is holding these and so many other companies back? Boards without women should be a thing of the past.

As more corporations take on the civic responsibilities and focus on purpose and ESG, a board without women is asking for trouble with just about everybody: consumers, shareholders, employees, and social activists. Why not seat people on your board who are committed to putting even more women and minorities in the corporate boardroom? As a result of their personal, social, and business experience, groups of diverse individuals are tuned into varied issues that ultimately may have an impact on a company's profitability. By virtue of their diversity, they are likely to be good at picking up on subtleties and nuances that can signal future problems.

CHAPTER 3

"BUT WE ALREADY HAVE A WOMAN"—UH, NOT SO FAST!

Unity, not uniformity, must be our aim. We attain unity only through variety. Differences must be integrated, not annihilated, not absorbed.

—MARY PARKER FOLLETT

D etermining the best composition for your board is never an easy task. And incidentally, given that companies are not static, board composition should not be static either.

As mentioned earlier, all too many companies seated their first qualified woman only recently, and as far as some are concerned, it is "one and done." These companies believe that with the presence of a lone woman on a board of directors, they can put a checkmark next to the diversity box.

What they can put a checkmark next to is, in fact, tokenism. And as with any halfhearted attempt at rectifying a social injustice or business misstep, it is too little and often too late. What some companies do not understand is that this is not a compliance exercise, this is a business imperative.

The dearth of women on corporate boards is at the very least a public relations embarrassment for companies whose toothpaste, perfume, clothing, laptops, pharmaceuticals, gasoline, mortgages, home-care services, and software are most often purchased by women. Favorably for some, the visibility of this situation is limited because many consumers do not understand boards and don't pay much attention to this somewhat opaque and misunderstood function within organizations.

Nevertheless, some companies do succumb to pressure from negative media attention, activist shareholders, or women's groups to seat a token woman at the boardroom table. Sounds like a good start, right?

At least three women on a board of directors helps create the critical mass necessary for women to share ideas, posit alternatives, and yes, disagree.

As some of these token female board directors have told me, the one-woman-per-board mindset often indicates a board every bit as resistant to alternate points of view as a completely male board. A lone individual, whether male or female, finds it challenging to speak up in a group dominated by the opposite sex. Indeed, research shows that all of us take cues from our environment, and if we sense that our voices are not welcome, we muffle them. As far back as 1969, two French psychologists—one male, one female—published a paper summarizing the results of an experiment that showed how groupthink shapes an individual's willingness to express an opinion, especially if it goes against the consensus of the crowd. "While reacting with other persons, the person reacts to them … by tempering his judgments so as to avoid the possibility of being extremely different from others," the authors wrote.[51]

Global nonprofit Catalyst reports that the presence of at least three women on a board of directors helps create the critical mass necessary for women to share ideas, posit alternatives, and yes, disagree. And ultimately make a positive contribution. What Facebook COO Sheryl Sandberg told Wharton professor Adam Grant underscores what women on boards have told me time and time again: "When a woman speaks in a professional setting, she walks a tightrope. Either she's barely heard, or she's judged as too aggressive. When a man says virtually the same thing, heads nod in appreciation for his fine idea. As a result, women often decide that saying less is more."[52]

Think for a moment about the times you have been the lone man in a situation. The lone American. The lone English speaker. The lone husband in a women's clothing store. The very attributes that bolster your identity in your everyday life suddenly make you feel out of place. How can that be? You are proud of your masculinity, your nationality, your language. But once you encounter a room full of the "other," you become hyperconscious. You are different. If only you had somebody like you around!

Research into the status of a minority subgroup within a larger dominant group is not new. It goes back to the mid-1950s when social psychologist Solomon Asch conducted an experiment to investigate the extent to which social pressure by a majority affects an individual's independent thinking. Using a study group of fifty male students from Swarthmore College, Asch put one student in a room with seven confederates (people in on Asch's experiment) and asked all of them to compare the length of lines in a vision test. Asch instructed his seven confederates to give an incorrect answer in twelve of the eighteen trials. He measured the number of times each of the test subjects conformed to the majority view. On average, about one-third of the students conformed to the majority that gave clearly wrong answers. Asch also ran a control group in which none of the confederates colluded with him to give intentionally incorrect answers. In that test, less than 1 percent of the students gave the wrong answer.[53]

So it is easy to see how a majority can influence the thinking of a lone individual—and how a lone individual can be swayed into passivity or acquiescence, even if it means making an error.

Fast-forward to 2011, when a group of researchers published a paper on the impact of one, two, and three women on corporate boards.[54] Drawing on their work with Norwegian corporate boards, and on research done in the years since Asch's conformity experiment, they found that the presence of one woman confirmed what Asch discovered in his experiment at Swarthmore: A lone individual can be cowed into going along with the group. These researchers found, too, that the contributions of female directors to company innovation become evident "when the critical mass (at least three women directors) is reached."

There is strength in numbers. Women—and minorities—learn early and fast that their lone presence on a board may be a grudging concession to some corporate diversity compliance initiative. They conclude that boards see inclusiveness as not a real benefit but rather one forced on them by the women's movement or some other social good initiative. Newly arrived women board members have told me that they get an unspoken message to stay quiet during board meetings. "I have to sort of sit at the end of the table, at least until I gain some seniority," says a woman I placed on a large consumer products board. "It's expected of me to toe the line, not push back too hard, and go along to get along." Despite her having been brought on, in effect, to shake things up, the lone female board member may not have much of a voice.

Often it is the small things that create cohesiveness and build relationships. The lone woman board director can be further silenced during something as ordinary as a bio break. "The men go to the bathroom together and chum it up along the way," the same woman told me. "I go to the ladies' room by myself."

Bonding, so crucial to board relationships, cannot happen if you have no one with whom to bond. We all know the power of informal communications and the way that relationships can get built and solidified in the most innocuous of ways.

Many male board directors see diversity initiatives as nice to have, not need to have. When the California State Assembly passed non-binding Resolution 62 in 2013 to "encourage equitable and diverse gender representation on corporate boards,"[55] and to urge the inclusion of at least three women per nine-member board between January 2014 and December 2016, I thought, "Great. Now is the time to call a male board member I know at a company headquartered in California. Surely, he will be concerned about the lack of women on his board."

I was so naïve.

"It's not the law," he told me, when I talked to him about the resolution. "Frankly, we have other things to worry about. Like, we have a business to run!"

Resolution 62 cited numerous studies, from McKinsey and Company's "Women Matter" to the research paper on Norwegian boards cited previously, but this director wrote it off as social arm-twisting, not a business necessity. And *he* does not have to worry about being alone. The chair of the California Senate Select Committee on Women, Work and Families held a hearing in August 2017—three years after the California Assembly's passage of Resolution 62—to discuss women's continued underrepresentation at every level of corporate leadership compared to men. "Although [Senate Concurrent Resolution] 62 intended to encourage companies to add women to their boards, it appears they are falling short in doing so,"[56] State Senator Hannah-Beth Jackson (D-Santa Barbara) wrote on her website.

Many respond to the question about lack of diversity on their boards with a comment like "our business is doing so well anyway." To which I reply, "How well could you be doing if you were to follow best practices?"

Indeed, it may have been just this inertia that in September 2018 led California to become the first state in America to pass a law requiring companies with headquarters in that state to have women on their boards. More on this later.

Corporate boards are as prone to complacency as anybody else, and realistically speaking, they may not be motivated to change if they do not have to. And why would they? Until recently boards were made up mostly of men and most did not question this. Women and minorities were believed to be token concessions to government overreach and grassroots social pressure.

"Due to their under-representation in the group, [women and minorities] are viewed as a symbol or token," wrote the authors of the Norwegian board study. Citing research conducted in the 1970s and 1980s, the study authors concluded that for the board tokens themselves, "stereotyping could result in the perception of barriers to exerting influence on decisions in the group. Moreover, tokens are perceived negatively, sometimes with downright derision and are often doubted and not trusted; as a result, being labelled as a token often creates discomfort, isolation and self-doubt."[57]

By now you might be thinking: "Why doesn't an accomplished woman with something to say just speak up? If she has a good idea, the group will reward her for it."

That is not what the research says.

A team of university and US Army researchers—three men and one woman—in 2017 studied the perception that managers have of female and male leadership in a collaborative setting. Expanding on earlier research done by others, the authors operated on the premise that "men's assertive behaviors are often seen as more legitimate and as adding more value to the group than are women's similar behaviors."[58] Consequently, they expected that group members would evaluate men who speak up as acting "more legitimately than women who do so because assertive, change-oriented behaviors are more in line with gendered expectations for men."

Put in brutal terms, people take what men say seriously. Less so with women.

The team's research study involved thirty-six United States Military Academy (USMA) teams competing in an annual two-day military skills competition. Teams had to have at least one woman, and on average had two. The study results offered up no real surprises. They indicated that "the types of voice people provide, and their gender significantly interact to influence their leader emergence through the accrual (or not) of status." That is, whether a speaker had a "promotive" voice that encouraged positive action to change the workplace for the better, or a "prohibitive" voice that cautioned against taking a specific workplace action, people far and away viewed male speakers as the group leaders.

Put in brutal terms, people take what men say seriously. Less so with women.

Anecdotal evidence bears out the same conclusion. Two *Harvard Business Review* (*HBR*) authors wrote in 2013 about a lone female board member who felt routinely "shut out and stifled during meetings"[59]—this despite her status as an acknowledged expert in the financial services industry. "Her questions were greeted not with respectful collegiality but as intrusions into the 'real' conversation among the male board members," the authors wrote.

These *HBR* authors asked the male board members in their study to list the four types of obstacles they believe women face:

- limited access to and acceptance on boards because of weaker networks and the old boys' club

- lack of experience and industry knowledge

- bias and prejudice

- having to work harder to prove themselves

They also asked female board members to list four obstacles they believe women face:

- not being heard and listened to

- not being accepted as an equal or as part of the "in" group

- establishing credibility

- stereotyped expectations of women's behavior

Patrice Merrin, who has served in C-level positions in the Canadian mining and healthcare industries, tries to turn adverse stereotypes into boardroom fortune.

"Knowing that I am always the 'outsider' and diversity board member forces me to figure out, first, how can I get on the board of my choice, and second, how am I going to contribute to a company's performance," she says.

Merrin has told me that even as CEO of a successful mining company, she did not get one invitation to be on a board of any kind.

"Unless you are a chartered accountant or something that is easily labeled, people don't know what to do with you," Merrin said. "Unless you're a man. A woman can have deep expertise in one sector or broad expertise in several. She can be in the contract bridge hall of fame and speak fluent Mandarin, English, and Tagalog, but when it comes to giving her a seat on a board, she is somehow not digestible. Meanwhile, none of the men are expected to have five accomplishments on their CV."

Determined to sit on a board, Merrin approached companies in Paris and London on her own initiative.

"In Canada I was a nothing burger," she told me. "I felt like a supplicant, like, 'please notice me!' But in Europe, where most countries have a 30 percent quota for female board membership, recruiters were happy to meet with me." Not everyone—male or female—has the chutzpah Merrin exhibited.

Like Merrin, a private investor, entrepreneur, and independent board member who has chosen to remain anonymous came up with work-arounds to get herself on a corporate board.

"In neither of my first two board searches was I recruited through an official recruiting process," she says. "It was through my personal network that I was identified as being appropriate."

Indeed, this executive says, she has never witnessed the use of an official search firm recruiting process to place a board member. "What I've come to believe is that the limited number of women on boards is not a supply issue, but rather a network issue," she says. "Simply by being at the right social engagement at the right time, and talking to the vice chair of a board, did I end up the only woman—and only African American—on the board of a beauty products company."

"No CEO is going to put somebody in the boardroom unless they really know who that person is," she says. "They're not going to choose a person from a résumé or a LinkedIn profile."

As I mentioned earlier, only 30 percent of board searches are done through executive search organizations. For that reason, this director and numerous others have described helping advance diversity by keeping their own list of board qualified women and minorities. Thus, when they get the call and do not have capacity themselves, they can make a well-thought-through suggestion and thereby increase the probability of a diverse candidate being appointed to the board. It is these individual organic efforts that make a difference. As they say, it takes a village. "In a worst-case scenario, I'll arrange a meeting between the CEO and my candidate, and then my candidate at least will be on the corporate radar," she says. "Of course, that's more easily said than done. Actually, getting a CEO or board member to meet somebody they don't know is itself a herculean task."[60]

* * *

Tokenism in the C-suite and the boardroom has brought neither balance nor diversity to the strategic decision-making process. Companies miss out on the richness and wisdom of people who have unique life experiences and unique perspectives. The placement of a lone woman at a boardroom table full of men may work in the rare instance. But it is simply not enough.

I am not arrogant enough to say I have found the silver bullet for superior corporate performance. I can say, though, that research into corporate systems shows that a board with at least 30 percent female board directors—usually three women—contributes to an environment in which women feel comfortable enough to speak up. Indeed, research by Catalyst has shown that companies with more women board directors experience higher financial performance—and that "three or more [women] may be the charm."[61] The Peterson Institute for International Economics, found that boards with 30 percent or more women could add up to 6 percent to their net margins.[62]

I can say that a study conducted by the Network of Executive Women, Accenture, and Mercer finds that "firms with no women in C-suite or board positions that increased female representation to 30 percent saw a 1-percentage-point increase in net margin, equal to a 15-percent increase in profitability."[63]

I can get behind the conclusion drawn by management researchers that "reaching a critical number of women directors is desirable because it not only affects the nature of group interactions, but also increases the diversity of viewpoints within a group."[64]

I can assert that female representation aids in the formation of good corporate governance. As one European Union study put it, "Women are perceived to be more conscientious in performing their tasks, more risk-averse both in investing their own assets and in investing on behalf of others, and more other-oriented."[65]

You can hear the bewilderment in a 2016 Harvard School of Public Health article urging the inclusion of more than one woman on a corporate board: "Women earn 57 percent of bachelor's degrees, over 62 percent of master's degrees, and 53 percent of degrees such as PhDs, medical degrees, and law degrees in the United States. This means that there is a large talent pool of women who can greatly add to your workforce, not just in terms of their gender, but in the range of experiences and competencies that they can bring to your organization."[66] Why then haven't corporate boards expanded their search for some highly credentialed women, who could contribute fresh ideas, inspire better company performance, and broaden the talent pool at the top of the company?

When I ask directors to add a woman to their board, they often tell me, "But we already have one woman!"

I say, "But you have seven men!"

Board diversity is not a compliance exercise. It is the right thing to do.

Above all else, it is simply good for business.

An analysis of boards in companies on the Financial Times Stock Exchange (FTSE) found that operational performance and share prices were both higher in companies where women made up over 20 percent of board members than in those with lower female representation.[67]

Professional services company Grant Thornton made a convincing argument in 2015 when it studied corporate diversity in the US, UK, and India and concluded that companies with male-only boards forego $655 billion in profits.[68]

"The status quo is the product of a bygone era," writes Grant Thornton's Francesca Lagerberg. She points to research from the Kellogg School of Management, which shows that diversity within a group "creates awkwardness, and the need to diffuse this tension leads to better group problem solving."[69]

One female board director can be "put in her place" by delegitimizing her input. But genuine board diversity—with at least three female directors—"changes the flow of the process and makes people stop and pay attention."[70]

And as the Kellogg researchers discovered, the true beneficiaries of the female "newcomers" were not the women but rather the existing—male—board members. "Instead, the behavior and feelings of old-timers who agreed with newcomers (i.e., opinion allies to the newcomer) had a larger impact on the groups' outcomes," they write. "The results add to the idea that surface-level (i.e., social) diversity may ultimately be beneficial for groups even when out-group members do not bring different deep-level task perspectives to the group."[71]

Board diversity is good for everybody.

Men included.

It is time to bridge the gap between qualified women seeking a board seat and executives and board directors in a position to recruit them.

If you have one woman on your board, leverage your advantage by adding another.

And another.

It is the right thing to do for your business results. And incidentally, stakeholders including your investors, employees, and customers will notice.

CHAPTER 4

SORRY, BUT VERNON JORDAN CAN'T BE YOUR ONLY CHOICE

Diversity is about all of us, and about us having to figure out how to walk through this world together.

—JACQUELINE WOODSON

Vernon Jordan was quite popular back in the 1980s. If a corporation or not-for-profit group sought a Black man for a board seat, this American businessman, attorney, and civil rights activist was often the go-to choice.

Jordan grew up in segregated Atlanta in the 1950s and attended DePauw University as the only Black student in a class of four hundred. After graduating from Howard University Law School, he worked alongside fellow civil rights activists to sue the University of Georgia for racial discrimination—a successful suit that resulted in the admission of two Black teenagers who went on to become journalist Charlayne Hunter-Gault and orthopedic physician Hamilton E. Holmes. From the earliest days in his career, Jordan devoted himself to helping other Black people acquire the educational and professional opportunities that had made his life financially and intellectually rewarding.

Given all that, surely, he must have been affronted by the notion that in 1998 he was one of the few Black people that corporate America considered qualified to occupy a board seat. And not just one seat, but ten: American Express, Bankers Trust New York Corp., Callaway Golf Co., Dow Jones & Co., JC Penney Co., Revlon, Ryder System, Inc., Sara Lee Corp., Union Carbide Corp., and Xerox Corp.[72]

All at the same time.

Proponents of good governance would be interested to know that eight of Jordan's ten boards were also clients of his law firm, Akin, Gump, Strauss, Hauer & Feld LLP. Additionally, these ten boards meant that Jordan had eighty-four board meetings per year with fifty-seven committee meetings. Even if he made every meeting—and apparently his attendance was on target everywhere except at Bankers Trust and Dow Jones—how could he possibly be attuned to the intricacies and nuances of ten different companies in ten different industries? Even if he had nothing else going on in his life (which was not the case), it would have been a challenge to govern this conglomeration—no matter how brilliant he may have been.

The takeaway for Vernon Jordan? Many directors and corporations must not have known any other Black people. Or, as reported in *The Washington Post* in 1998, "current and former executives and directors of Fortune 500 companies who have worked with Jordan say his presence on so many boards results in large part from the paucity of 'qualified' African American representatives."[73]

This was 1998. Not ancient history.

In fact, it was 1964 when the first two Black people were ever elected to a corporate board: Samuel R. Pierce Jr. to the board of U.S. Industries and insurance magnate Asa T. Spaulding to W.T. Grant Co. By 1987 there were eighty Black directors in the Fortune 500, of which twenty-four sat on three or more boards.[74]

Today, there is still a tendency to "pull a Vernon Jordan." Only this time it is Richard Parsons, the former chairman of Citigroup and Time Warner, or Kenneth Chenault, former CEO of American Express. Shirley Jackson, President of Rensselaer Polytechnic Institute and the first Black woman to receive a PhD from MIT, has been another diversity standard bearer. Until recently, almost every time a company requested a Black woman, Jackson was on the short list. Not to take anything away from these extremely accomplished individuals, but we have 47.8 million Black people in the US—14.6 percent of the total population, according to the 2018 US Census.[75] Too many corporate boards are recycling the same Black directors, and they represent a fraction of the talent that exists in the Black executive echelon. This high "recycle rate" serves to increase diversity but limit the pool of new contenders for board seats.

Despite the many lists of qualified Black executives that circulate in the corporate halls of power and articles extolling accomplishments and progress, in 2019 Black Enterprise Registry reported 322 Black corporate directors in the S&P 500 and a mere twenty-one Black chairmen and lead directors. Additionally, a full 37 percent of the S&P 500 did not have any Black board members. And lest you think this phenomenon is disappearing, this number was 39 percent in 2017.[76]

What is going on here?

The answer: it is complicated. But let me summarize.

We in the board recruiting world use a term *board ready*. We ask if a candidate is board ready, which can mean, do they have enough seniority and the right kind of seniority? Do they have gravitas and influence? We see over and over again a misguided belief that females and underrepresented minorities who are board ready are in short supply.

In part, what is going on is a bad case of complacency. It takes effort to look for new talent. It takes more effort to determine whether someone who has not previously sat on a board is board ready. The endeavor is important because if we are to change the situation, we must be able to rely on trusted advisors such as our search partners to be able to identify, access, assess, and recruit new and previously untested board directors. This, of course, is not to take away from the experienced and wonderful diverse directors already sitting on boards. I simply want to emphasize the fact that there is a wealth of talent out there ready to serve on boards. While it's easier to just go with the tried and true, sometimes this strategy can be suboptimal.

Boards need to go beyond their belief that only CEOs and former CEOs make good directors.

Another issue is that boards need to go beyond their belief that only CEOs and former CEOs make good directors. As of 2018, there were only three Black CEOs in the Fortune 500. Three! Today there are four.

Only three Black women have ever been CEO of an S&P 500 company—Ursula Burns at Xerox, Mary Winston as an interim CEO at Bed Bath & Beyond, and newly anointed Rosalind Brewer at Walgreens. The belief that only CEOs make for board directors perpetuates exclusion. We need, of course, to fix diversity in the C-suite, and concurrently boards must look to functional experts such as chief financial officers, chief operating officers, chief marketing officers, chief digital officers, chief information officers, division presidents, and the like. Every board needs a variety of skills and expertise, and no board needs to consist solely of CEOs and former CEOs.

What we have is a dual phenomenon of overboarding—seating one individual on an excessive number of boards—and underboarding, in which hundreds of S&P 500 companies seem not to acknowledge the absence of Black views and experiences as consumers, employees, managers, executives, and investors.

Not too long ago, I was working on a board search for a company that requested a "diversity candidate." Kudos to the CEO and the board for recognizing the need for a Black director at a company with a high number of Black employees. This was to be the first non-Caucasian on this board. My colleagues and I presented the company with many qualified individuals. My personal choice was a West Coast–based Black male executive. He had relevant and excellent experience, as well as a great education and fabulous style. He was board ready. Great on paper. Great in person. Triple A pick.

He met the board of directors. Everyone was impressed by him.

Except for the CEO. All he was supposed to do was have a brief meet-and-greet with the candidate by phone, but he basically ended up grilling him. And what bothered the CEO about this prospect? Two things. He was two minutes late for their introductory call. And the candidate asked a question that rubbed the CEO the wrong way. Probably asked him something tough that he did not want to answer. The candidate was supersmart that way.

"I do not want this guy on my board," he said.

Of course not. He asked questions. He was going to push back if pushing back was warranted. He was not the yes man that some CEOs would like.

As for the other board members, they deferred to the CEO. They took the easy way out and pulled him from the search process.

I have thought a lot about that CEO's reaction to this terrific board candidate. Was the CEO reasonably holding him to a high standard, or was he in the grip of unconscious bias?

Unconscious (or implicit) bias is a verifiable phenomenon. The Kirwan Institute for the Study of Race and Ethnicity at Ohio State University defines implicit bias as,

> the attitudes or stereotypes that affect our understanding, actions, and decisions in an unconscious manner. These biases, which encompass both favorable and unfavorable assessments, are activated involuntarily and without an individual's awareness or intentional control. Residing deep in the subconscious, these biases are different from known biases that individuals may choose to conceal for the purposes of social and/or political correctness. Rather, implicit biases are not accessible through introspection.[77]

Nearly thirty years ago social psychologist Patricia Devine argued that racial stereotypes can influence people's behavior without their awareness or intent.[78] The Kirwan Institute states that implicit biases are pervasive and everyone possesses them. Naturally, I had to question the intensity of the CEO's opposition to a Black executive based on what I took to be inconsequential. So while many companies may claim to want more diversity on their board, it is critical to examine and be realistic about the reasons that this goal is not reached.

Science supports my skepticism. Research studies have demonstrated bias across nearly every field and for many different groups of people: Latino patients get less pain medication than White patients; elderly women receive fewer life-saving interventions than elderly men, and Black students are more likely to be punished than White students who have misbehaved in the same way.[79]

It is precisely because everybody has unconscious or implicit biases that forward-thinking boards are introducing the National Football League's Rooney Rule[80] into the director selection process. The Rooney Rule, adopted in 2003, by the NFL originally required teams to interview ethnic minority candidates for head coaching jobs. Today this has expanded to include general manager positions as well. Within the context of businesses, the Rooney Rule can be applied at any level. A tremendous application of the Rooney Rule has been embarked upon by the New York City Comptroller's Office in their multiyear initiative, the Board Accountability Project. The overall initiative began in 2014, and in phase 3.0 (November 2019) Comptroller Scott Stringer sent letters to fifty-six S&P 500 companies that do not have a Rooney Rule policy, regardless of their existing level of diversity at the board and CEO level. Letters calling for the Rooney Rule to be implemented were sent to such companies as Activision Blizzard, Berkshire Hathaway, Ford Motor Company, and Walmart.

The Rooney Rule applied to board recruiting is certainly progress. But I have seen how it may not be enough. When presenting a company with a long list of board candidates that includes one or even several diverse candidates, the tendency is to skip over them in favor of those who are part of the majority. The simple fix for this is a list that contains only diverse candidates if and when diversity is requested. It should go without saying that everyone on said list is qualified first and also happens to be diverse. Research reported in *Harvard Business Review* found that more than one Black coach for an NFL coaching position needs to be interviewed to increase the number of Black coaches actually hired.[81]

Companies may also believe that adding an unknown person to the board is risky—because they may rock the boat. Thus, a known entity is thought to be a safe bet. But is it?

Effective corporate governance actually means appointing board members willing to do a little boat rocking. A board's impact is minimal if it acts "only as a necessary legal entity tolerated by the chairman," corporate governance experts Jay W. Lorsch and Martin Lipton wrote in 1992. "On the other hand, a board can contribute a great deal if it acts as a truly diverse group of informed and interested counsellors, advisors and directors of management."[82]

Diversity is not only, or primarily, about skin color and even gender identity. It is about a mindset.

I have seen it many times: conformity and collegiality are often a precondition for joining a board. Appointing another docile board director even if he/she is ethnically diverse is problematic. They do not truly increase diversity. This is because diversity is not only, or primarily, about skin color and even gender identity. It is about a mindset. Truly engaging Black people in the boardroom means being receptive to the insights of a group of people with a range of personal and social experiences that many members of the group in power have *not* shared, historically and psychologically. Installing a don't-rock-the-boat "diverse" director on any board is really a way of keeping true diversity of thought out of the boardroom.

* * *

Returning to the start of this chapter, the historical reliance on a handful of tried-and-true diverse directors is counterproductive for all. The role of board director is complex and increasingly time consuming. All the way back in 1992, business attorneys and previously mentioned corporate governance experts Martin Lipton and Jay W. Lorsch wrote, "Based on our experience, the most widely shared problem [that] directors have is a lack of time to carry out their duties. Directors rarely spend as much as a working day together in and around each meeting. Further, in many boardrooms too much of this limited time is occupied with reports from management and various formalities. In essence, the limited time outside directors have together is not used in a meaningful exchange of ideas among themselves or with management/inside directors."[83]

In April 2019, Vanguard updated its director overboarding policy. It stated that it would vote against active executives (those still working in a full-time role) sitting on more than one outside public company board (so a total of two public company boards). Vanguard will vote against any director (actively working or not) who serves on five or more public company boards.[84] BlackRock states a variation of this: public-company CEOs may sit on one outside board in addition to their own board. Everyone else may sit on three outside boards as well as their own.[85] Any more than this and the director is considered over-committed. At the time of writing, in the US there are 197 directors who serve on five or more public-company boards. And this does not take into account private company boards and nonprofits.

Despite this, I am glad to say that the overboarding phenomenon has been on the decline for the past twenty years.

Overboarding is responsible for yet another strike against diversity candidates. When corporate executives hold on to multiple boardroom seats, they effectively keep everybody else out.

* * *

As the old saying goes, "actions speak louder than words." Regarding racial inequality and injustice, in 2020 in America we have had much of both. Many actions, many words. We seemed to finally be at an inflection point when the status quo is no longer acceptable. Our country questioned long-held beliefs (both conscious and unconscious) about the lives and treatment of the Black community.

There is much that can be done and hopefully the collective efforts of many will lead to change. Statements against racial injustice and discussions as to how to make change are certainly a necessary start. But we should be challenging corporations and ourselves to change the composition of boards to fully represent the demographics of where they are located. This is of course true for boardrooms and should extend to the C-suite as well, since it serves as the "feeder system" for boardrooms.

For this to work properly, in addition to the fundamental building blocks previously mentioned in this chapter, as a society and business community, we must also address the pipeline of board directors. The pipeline of board directors is made up of those coming up the ranks. Regardless of the type of expertise we are looking for in our next director, the prerequisite is seniority and experience as a leader. To improve the pipeline of diverse directors, therefore, we must make sure that we look to earlier stages of careers and understand roadblocks to the executive ranks. We must understand what prevents people from advancing in their careers. What are the obstacles? A recent study titled "Being Black in Corporate America" found that most Black professionals experienced prejudice at work. Furthermore, this prejudice was reported as highest in the Midwest and lowest in the Northeast.[86]

It is often said that any discussion of diversity is incomplete without a discussion of inclusion. It is also said that diversity initiatives are doomed to failure if inclusion is not part of the equation. It is one thing to hire people of different races and genders; it is quite another to have a culture and environment that welcomes these people in their entirety. The Society for Human Resources Management states that "to get workplace diversity and inclusion right, you need to build a culture where everyone feels valued and heard."[87]

An organization that focuses on both diversity and inclusion appreciates that getting diversity in the door is only a start. This must be followed by retention and promotion for those who are particularly talented and competent. Once we understand this, we must be realistic and objective about bottlenecks and stumbling blocks. If we can create work environments that foster a feeling that opportunity is open to all and success is based on merit, we can incentivize people to try their best. Only then can we expect those that forge ahead to be heterogenous and not of a predetermined "type."

Narratives about racial inequality and injustice or the value of diversity are only the start. This must be followed by consistent efforts and actions that are measurable and demonstrable. It is time to move beyond endless conversations, trainings, and preparation. We need to move beyond simply releasing statements about one tragedy or another. Diversity in the boardroom should not be a knee-jerk reaction. As we know "a fish rots from the head," and it is incumbent on boards to continue to diversify themselves.

CHAPTER 5

ASIAN AMERICANS: GAINING ENTRY ALBEIT SLOWLY

No culture can live if it attempts to be exclusive.

—MAHATMA GANDHI

I t is a dumbfounding paradox that Asian Americans are under-represented on North American corporate boards at a time when China, India, South Korea, and other Asian countries are global economic powerhouses. It is incredible that in most discussions on board and corporate diversity, Asians are not even mentioned.

The US Asian population grew 72 percent between 2000 and 2015 (from 11.9 million to 20.4 million), the fastest growth rate of any major racial or ethnic group. "Looking forward, Asians are projected to become the largest immigrant group in the country. In 50 years, Asians will make up 38 percent of all US immigrants."[88]

Statistics indicate that Asian Americans are a significant part of the US economy. In fact, nearly 7 percent of all businesses in the US are Asian-owned, though Asians account for only 5.8 percent of the eighteen-or-older population.[89] And importantly, in 2016 alone, they spent $825 billion on goods and services—representing the third-largest spending power of all multicultural groups.[90] In 2015 the median annual household income of households headed by Asian Americans was $73,060, compared with $53,600 among all US households.[91]

Despite their presence in virtually every sector of the economy, Asian Americans are nearly absent in C-suites and boardrooms of large companies. Some 77.2 percent of Fortune 500 companies have no Asian American board representation whatsoever.[92] According to Deloitte and The Alliance for Board Diversity, Asian/Pacific Islanders hold 3.7 percent of Fortune 500 board seats.[93] This has been referred to as a corporate blind spot. "Because Asian Americans are not considered an underrepresented minority, they are given little priority or attention in diversity programs."[94] There is also the "model minority" stereotype that persists for Asian Americans. This stereotype characterizes "Asian Americans as inherently successful and problem-free, particularly in contrast to other minority groups."[95]

Even in Silicon Valley, where Asian Americans compose 27.2 percent of the high-tech workforce, they hold only 13.9 percent of executive and board positions.[96] It has been reported that while Asian Americans may be hired in large numbers by tech companies, they are the group least likely to be promoted into managerial and executive ranks. Whites are twice as likely as Asians to hold executive positions. And while White women have made gains over the past decade as more have broken through the glass ceiling, Asian women have not experienced the same. In fact, they are among those least likely to be promoted, and their gap with White men has worsened over the last decade.[97] It is interesting to note, though, that in 2019, of the five Asian CEOs in the largest companies in the US, four of them were running technology companies: Satya Nadella (Microsoft), Sundar Pichai (Google), John Chen (Blackberry), and

The history of Asians in the US is chock-full of bias and repudiation.

Shantanu Narayen (Adobe). The fifth is Ajay Banga of Mastercard. In 2020 Arvind Krishna joined these ranks when he took over as CEO of IBM.

Historians and social researchers have tried to make sense of how Asian Americans made a relatively rapid ascent into the American middle and upper classes without having become more influential in the executive sphere. To better understand the origins of this phenomenon it helps to look at a bit of history.

The history of Asians in the US is chock-full of bias and repudiation. Recall that the Chinese Exclusion Act, signed by President Chester A. Arthur in 1882, set an absolute ten-year moratorium on Chinese labor immigration on grounds that the Chinese "endangered the good order of certain localities."[98] The "Chinese Must Go" movement was so strong that Chinese immigration to the United States declined from 39,500 in 1882 to only 10 in 1887. And Japanese Americans were forcibly relocated to internment camps during World War II, even while relatively few German Americans or Italian Americans suffered the same fate.[99] It is horrifying to consider that 62 percent of the Japanese internees were US citizens.[100] Many South-Asian Indian immigrants originally went to Canada to work on the railroad and then migrated to the United States. The Center for Global Education at Asia Society has stated "this was decried as a 'Hindu invasion' by exclusionists and white labor, the 'tide of the Turbans' was outlawed in 1917 when Congress declared that India was part of the Pacific-Barred Zone of excluded Asian countries."[101]

Even today there are a variety of generalizations and misperceptions that may serve to exclude Asians from the boardrooms of corporate America.

Firstly, the mere categorization of Asian or Asian American or even Asian/Pacific Islander is an oversimplification and ignores the nuances and vast differences in this population. The US Asian community consists of more than fifty racial/ethnic groups that speak over thirty languages. Massive diversity within a community that is often bunched together. Trying to understand why Asian Americans are missing from corporate boardrooms is a simplification. In fact, it has been shown that there are stark differences in levels of success in corporate America between Asians of certain regions and countries versus others. Jackson G. Lu of MIT's Sloan School of Management, Richard E. Nisbett of the University of Michigan, and Michael W. Morris of Columbia University's Business School published a study in which they found that East Asians are less likely than South Asians (from India, Pakistan, and Bangladesh) or White Americans to advance to leadership positions in American companies. As a percentage of their portion of the total US population, South Asians even outper-formed White Americans.[102]

With over fifty racial/ethnic groups comprising Asian Americans, trying to identify some universal element of culture or character that hinders their progress into boardrooms will not yield answers. Indeed, the previously mentioned study by Lu, Nisbett, and Morris found that East Asians (e.g., Chinese) were less likely than South Asians (e.g., Indians) and Whites to attain leadership positions, whereas South Asians were more likely than Whites to do so. At the same time, East Asians were found to experience less prejudice than South Asians, and the two groups were equally motivated by work and leadership. So, what is holding East Asians back? Interestingly, East Asians were found to be lower in assertiveness. The authors concluded, "These results suggest that East Asians hit the bamboo ceiling because their low assertiveness is incongruent with American norms concerning how leaders should communicate. The bamboo ceiling is not an Asian issue, but an issue of cultural fit."

What is noteworthy about this conclusion is that the very notion of assertiveness is not judged equally for everyone. Assertiveness is necessary for advancement through the ranks of companies. However, it has often been asserted (pardon the pun) that women's assertiveness is judged far more harshly than men. Women are often viewed as aggressive and bossy when asserting themselves, whereas similar behavior by men may be judged in a different light. Is it then possible that assertiveness among Asians and Asian Americans is judged by its own unique standard? Perhaps assertiveness is not lacking but rather must be tempered to assuage expectations?

Frequently referred to as the "model minority," Asians in this country are often perceived as hardworking but docile. "Many trace the invisibility of the community's challenges, in part, to the mythical characterization of the racial group as compliant, successful and faring well—tropes that have long obscured the reality of their struggles."[103]

On the other hand, it is an interesting paradox that all Asian Americans are thought to be raised by "Tiger Moms." Tiger Moms," or "Tiger Parenting," refers to strict and demanding parenting that requires hard work with little attention to individuality. As far as career success goes, both are excessive characterizations and neither particularly conducive to success in corporate America nor its boardrooms.

The tiger mom stereotype, popularized in large part by Amy Chua in *Battle Hymn of the Tiger Mother*, has gained traction in the media and may contribute to a picture of Asian American millennials as perfectionists and hyperambitious. CNBC reported in 2015 that "65 percent of Asian employees born after 1982 responded that they aimed to become the highest-ranked person at their current firm, compared to 45 percent of North Americans and 37 percent of Western Europeans of the same age." The report concludes condescendingly that "this surfeit of youthful ambition may need to be tempered if Asians are to achieve their dream of making it to the boardroom, because they risk missing key experiences along the way."[104]

A recent *Harvard Business Review* (*HBR*) piece suggests that persistent stereotypes about Asians have hamstrung their entry into the C-suite. On the one hand, Asian "competence" makes Asians appear "threatening"[105] in the workplace. On the other hand, social awkwardness makes them seem "unfit for leadership." The former quality engenders "admiration of and envy toward Asians"; the latter provokes "hostility toward and fear of Asians."

Well, which is it? Asians are too meek? Too nerdy? Too treacherous? Too ambitious? Too warped by their tiger moms?

Do Asians really have more issues than anybody else?

Stereotypes and misconceptions do tend to proliferate when there is a lack of information to counteract them. It is easy to misunderstand others if you have limited experience and exposure to them. This holds true for many groups and cultures. However, in the case of Asian Americans, there has been a well-documented dearth of representation in the media. The organization Asian Americans Advancing Justice (AAJC) states, "Asian Americans have historically been depicted in stereotypical, one-dimensional, and often dehumanizing ways by the media."[106] The population of regular Asian Pacific Islander American (APIA) actors on prime-time television amount to less than half of the actual APIA population percentage in the United States while White males remain the principal subjects of prime-time television.[107] The Asian Pacific American Media Coalition (APAMC) issues an annual report card on progress toward diversity and inclusion of Asian Pacific Americans (APAs) onscreen and behind the camera.[108] Most networks are still challenged in this way but the runaway success of the television show *Fresh Off the Boat* and the movie *Crazy Rich Asians* reflects some change in Hollywood. Ethnically diverse groups are finally getting a chance to tell their stories, and audiences are open to characters that go beyond historical stereotypes. This should go some way to changing the view of Asians from marginalized and typecast to central characters in media, in life, and eventually in corporate America and its boardrooms.

* * *

Many Asian Americans may be fed up with the stereotypes and simply start their own companies. Yet even here, Asian Americans face obstacles: some 83 percent of start-ups receiving venture capital funding are headed entirely by Caucasian founders, while only 12 percent of founders receiving VC funding are Asian.[109]

Asian Americans do not even seem to be on the radar of corporate boards in this country.

What do these absences tell us? Corporate America's conclusion may be that Asian Americans are doing "well enough." And as long as they are not stomping their feet outside the boardroom or executive suite, why rush to open the door to them? Perhaps corporate American has internalized the model minority myth? But it is absolutely time to part with it.

It's absurd: Asian Americans do not even seem to be on the radar of corporate boards in this country. When Asians are seated on a board, it is frequently because they come from a country in Asia or have on-the-ground experience there and they understand important regional business practices and the local marketplace. For a US company, this is largely meant to help expansion in this part of the world.

Latent in the model minority stereotype is the expectation of being hardworking and uncomplaining, and many have felt pressure to live up to the stereotype. This has meant that Asian Americans have not insisted on diversity representation, but this too is changing.

Ascend is the largest, nonprofit Pan-Asian organization for business professionals in North America. Ascend has a Pan-Asian board initiative to help increase the number of Asians on boards of US corporations. Leadership Education for Asian Pacifics (LEAP), a national nonprofit whose mission is to empower Asians and Pacific Islanders, is one quarter of the Alliance for Board Diversity. Together with the Executive Leadership Council, Catalyst, and the Hispanic Association on Corporate Responsibility, the Alliance for Board Diversity's goal is to enhance shareholder value by promoting inclusion of women and minorities on corporate boards.

Many are becoming more vocal about perceived exclusion and discrimination. For example, Ellen Pao is a Chinese American attorney and MBA. She is a former investment partner at Kleiner Perkins Caufield & Byers, a Silicon Valley venture capital firm and one of the most powerful and significant venture firms in the world. In 2012, Pao filed a gender discrimination lawsuit, charging that her employer rejected her promotion in favor of men whose workplace achievements were similar to hers. Although she found that she had all too few sympathizers and the jury exonerated Kleiner Perkins, Pao's suit brought to light something that many prefer not to talk about.[110] Students for Fair Admissions launched a lawsuit against Harvard University in 2014. They alleged that there is a substantial penalty against Asian Americans in the admission process. Although the judge ruled that Harvard does not discriminate against Asian Americans, this lawsuit also brought to light circumstances that previously had not been discussed in the mainstream. Shedding light on these concerns at least changes the conversation and forces many to think about these issues when they may not have previously. This awareness is the first step toward change.

* * *

Another bright spot in the move forward is the Board Accountability Project[111] (mentioned in the last chapter), launched in 2014 by New York City comptroller Scott Stringer to give shareowners the right to nominate directors at US companies, which will give them a stronger voice in corporate oversight. The belief is that this can be a catalyst for transformation on such issues as board diversity. In September 2017, Stringer sent a letter[112] to the nominating/governance committee chairs of companies held by the New York City Pension Funds, asking that they not limit the definition of board diversity to race and gender alone. They created a matrix—consisting of skills, experience, and demographic background on the y axis and board of director names on the x axis. While this tool has been used before, the one created by the Board Accountability Project is novel in that it breaks downs race/ethnicity with more specificity and, as such, sensitivity than typically seen on these tools. Rather than a simple catch all "diversity" category, there is "Asian, Hawaiian, or Pacific Islander" as one of six groups associated with "race/ethnicity." The fact that Asians are differentiated, as are "African American/Black," "White/Caucasian," "Hispanic/Latino," "Native American," and "Other" is a sign that ethnic diversity is complex and multifaceted. If we are to truly make progress in this area, we must appreciate the nuances in the categories we use and not simply go through a simple check-one-box compliance exercise.

It is worth noting that "excessive board tenure," a condition that contributes to the exclusion of women, Asian Americans, and other minority groups by keeping board seats filled with directors of long tenure, is one of the issues that Scott Stringer's diversity initiative seeks to address.[113] Stringer's Board Accountability Project recognizes that keeping any one individual seated for an "excessive" tenure—a decade or more, for example—ties up that seat and prevents a new executive with fresh thinking from coming on board.

The presence of Asian Americans in corporate boardrooms is long overdue.

That is an understatement, especially when you consider that *Time* magazine, an American journalistic icon, has been tracking the "high percentage of Asian tech employees and the disproportionately low percentage of Asian leaders"[114] since at least the late 1980s. As an Asian American high school teacher, interviewed by the magazine in 1987 and then reinterviewed in 2014, observed, "If you try to navigate the human part of it, we are seeing, as yellow people, our stereotypes still existing in the heads of many people. We don't get the chance to really go through and break the glass ceiling… We are putting limitations on our people."[115]

The more things change, the more they stay the same.

Isn't it time, at long last, for this minority to be part of the discussion on diversity and ultimately part of the change we are seeking?

CHAPTER 6

LGBTQ+: BRINGING THE RAINBOW TO THE BOARDROOM

Inclusivity means not 'just we're allowed to be there,' but we are valued. I've always said: smart teams will do amazing things, but truly diverse teams will do impossible things.

—CLAUDIA BRIND-WOODY

According to the 2019 Human Rights Campaign Foundation Corporate Equality Index, 572 US companies had a perfect equality score, meaning they could be designated a "Best Place to Work for LGBTQ+ equality."[116] To achieve this designation and receive a perfect equality score, these companies excelled in nondiscrimination policies, equitable benefits for LGBTQ+ employees and their families, and supported an inclusive culture and corporate social responsibility. These numbers and the programs and policies behind them are encouraging and demonstrate

If an organization is to be fully inclusive, diversity must begin at the top.

progress. However, as discussed in other chapters of this book, if an organization is to be fully inclusive, diversity must begin at the top.

As is often the case, industry leads the way to statutory tolerance, and there has been a long-standing commitment by many of the largest global corporations to ensure a nondiscriminatory work environment, domestic partner benefits to same-sex couples, and transgender-inclusive medical insurance.[117] Some of the companies that received the 2019 perfect equality score are Aramark Corp., Gilead Sciences, Inc., and The Kroger Company.

Until very recently the consensus has been that LGBTQ+ does not count as diversity—at least within the context of corporate governance. According to recent research by Out Leadership, "The vast majority of companies' basic board-diversity reporting guidelines have resisted the inclusion of LGBTQ+ identified metrics, often under the excuse of privacy. And today only twelve Fortune 500 companies mention sexual orientation and gender identity in their board diversity guidelines. Interestingly, however, thousands of companies globally do offer LGBTQ+ employees the opportunity to self-identify—just not at the board level."[118]

The reality is that members of the LGBTQ+ community do have different life experiences and, as a result, a different perspective that can be valuable to strategy and decision-making.

Many fervently support this view. A blog post I published on January 5, 2016, on LinkedIn, titled, "Diversity 5.0—LGBT in the Boardroom," for example, generated dozens of comments in support of my thesis that LGBTQ+ is diversity in its own right and merits attention and consideration in the boardroom.

From a military officer: "Physical, sexual preferences and gender are irrelevant. Treat everyone on a level field by not identifying anyone as anything other than a candidate."[119]

From an operations supervisor: "Family life, gender, race, none of this should be considered at all in the hiring process, and most of the time it can be deemed illegal to do so in the US."

From a project manager: "True diversity is where people are not judged by irrelevant criteria such as LGBT+ status."

These comments are well meaning. The problem is that when it comes to the public or corporate sphere, making too little of LGBTQ+ identity, oddly enough, bears the taint of the 1990s' "don't ask, don't tell" philosophy. If LGBTQ+ is nobody's business, and if it should be off-limits to discussion, then we cannot call it out as a special category whose members have unique insights and experiences that could benefit society, the workplace, and the corporate boardroom.

From the standpoint of corporate strategy and business performance, I see a big problem with pretending that being LGBTQ+ has no bearing on a person's professional life and that identification as a member of the LGBTQ+ community is not a genuine diversity category. In fact, the world is changing in so many dramatic ways that ignoring these nuances can be risky. Way back in 2016 J. Walter Thomson reported that only 48 percent of young people between the ages of thirteen and twenty years identify as 'exclusively heterosexual.' More recently it has been reported that 56 percent of young people do not exclusively buy clothing designed for their own gender and 56 percent of Gen Z says that they know someone firsthand who goes by gender neutral pronouns ("they," "them," or "ze").[120]

Although some may choose to keep their private lives private, for others, presenting an "inauthentic" self to one's colleagues and other stakeholders puts major limits on an honest and open business environment. The trickle down (up and sideways) effect is impossible to measure.

Some of the commenters on my blog post echo my point of view:

From a small business owner: "In this changed (of course, I mean for the better) world that we live in, I have traded in my phony chin and plastic smile for an actual representation of who I am."[121]

From a male clinical assistant professor: "When someone is planning the company event where I work, am I comfortable enough to say, 'Oh, my husband will attend'? Or will I resort to some covering pronoun or simply stay home?"

Turns out that faking it is a full-time job. And it is exhausting.

"Authentic leaders … work hard at developing self-awareness through persistent and often courageous self-exploration,"[122] according to Harvard Business School professor and former Medtronic CEO Bill George. "Denial can be the greatest hurdle that leaders face in becoming self-aware, but authentic leaders ask for, and listen to, honest feedback. They also use formal and informal support networks to help them stay grounded and lead integrated lives."[123]

LGBTQ+ is not simply about who you are attracted to but rather who you are.

In short, it may be a challenge to expect honesty or forthrightness from your colleagues or direct reports if you feel compelled to conceal an essential aspect of your identity. LGBTQ+ is not a monolithic group, and some individuals may not wish to reveal their sexualities. But for the 53 percent of LGBTQ+ employees in the US who are closeted in the workplace or the boardroom, many would want to come out because they believe it is the authentic thing to do. Others may still not feel ready or safe.

Just as skin color often reflects an individual's historical and psychological experience in the world, so does sexual orientation. LGBTQ+ is not simply about who you are attracted to but rather who you are. Straight people define themselves in relation to their families and significant others in a way that is about much more than sexual orientation, and the same is true for the LGBTQ+ community. To reduce being LGBTQ+ to one's sexual orientation is to simplify a complex and nuanced experience. Claudia Brind-Woody, vice president and managing director for global intellectual property licensing at IBM and cochair of the firm's global LGBT executive taskforce, has said that LGBTQ+ people want to engage authentically at work the same way straight people do. That is because people are the sum total of their life experiences, and if LGBTQ+ people have managed to get seated in the boardroom, the LGBTQ+ experience has contributed to their success. Why shouldn't every stakeholder know that?

* * *

Todd Sears learned from his own experience in the workplace that staying silent about his sexuality not only allowed colleagues to get away with bigoted remarks, but also resulted in his employer losing out on a billion-dollar market opportunity.

"In my first week at an investment banking firm, my boss used an antigay slur to talk about a colleague," says the US businessman and advocate for LGBTQ+ equality. "I had been out in college, but I got into the closet at work."[124]

Sears's decision to hide his sexuality only worked as a stopgap measure. He left the firm in less than a year.

"I committed myself to finding a place where I could be fully myself," he says.

Because Sears knew that the LGBTQ+ contribution to the US economy—more than $3.7 trillion—is bigger than the economies of Australia, Canada, and South Korea, he went on to build the first national private banking team on Wall Street that focuses on gay and lesbian clients. The group of financial advisors brought $1.4 billion in assets to his new firm.

Sears told me that he made a best practice out of LGBTQ+ openness when he started Out Leadership, a global LGBTQ+ business network that helps "out leaders and organizations realize the economic growth and talent dividend derived from inclusive business."[125] He had the same mission when he established Quorum, an Out Leadership project devoted to increasing representation of openly LGBTQ+ directors on corporate boards. Sears leveraged his Wall Street network to organize a business conversation in 2015 at Twitter's San Francisco headquarters, where keynote speakers included California Controller Betty T. Yee and California Insurance Commissioner Dave Jones. Lorrie Norrington of Lead Edge Capital, Jana Rich of Rich Talent Group, and Facebook's Alex Schultz participated in a lively panel discussion. More than one hundred LGBTQ+ executives and their "ally" supporters attended the global business community's "first-ever effort to get more LGBTQ+ people on corporate boards."[126]

Twitter's head of human resources got it.

"We look at communities of color and the LGBTQ+ community, and we always end up talking about the pipeline," he told the group. "Asking: Where is the talent, where are the candidates? To be in a room of senior leaders to discuss issues is amazing."

Would Twitter have recognized the potential return on investment of an LGBTQ+ marketplace if Todd Sears had continued to suffer institutionalized homophobic abuse in silence?

By speaking up, Sears ultimately used Out Leadership to create a network of more than nine hundred LGBTQ+ executives interested in board leadership.

In case that network did not go far enough, he also used Out Leadership in partnership with KPMG, to create a white paper called

"LGBT+ Board Diversity Guidelines," which encourages companies to include LGBT+ in their definition of board diversity. They recommend the following board diversity language:

> "Our Nominating and Governance Committee seeks to develop a Board that reflects diverse backgrounds, experiences, expertise, skill sets and viewpoints. We actively seek director candidates who bring diversity of age, gender, nationality, race, ethnicity, and sexual orientation."[127]

The organization worked closely with Amalgamated Bank to help make it the first nongovernmental institutional investor to expand the definition of corporate board diversity to include LGBTQ+ individuals.

Would Amalgamated Bank have reached out to the LGBTQ+ community if Todd Sears had chosen to remain silent for the rest of his working life?

"Saying that LGBTQ+ has no relevance in the boardroom is akin to saying that gender and race have no relevance there either," Sears told me. "That's an illogical assertion. For a company looking to best serve their employee base and their clients, LGBTQ+ inclusion at the board level will improve decision-making and send a signal that they truly care about diversity in all its forms."[128]

Sears's openness about his sexuality has inspired other LGBTQ+ business executives to be open as well. Trevor Burgess, CEO of C1 Financial, a Florida-based bank with thirty-one offices, says, "I need my board to look like my clients, because if my board looks like my clients, I can better serve them. The challenge is that not 100 per cent of the US is straight, white and male, and yet so many corporate boards still have mostly those characteristics."[129]

Openness—and openheartedness—characterizes former McDonald's chief operating officer and Papa John's current chief operating officer, Jim Norberg. "Education and knowledge are just powerful," he says. "I have seen so many minds changed through listening and dialogue."[130]

Norberg is happy to be seen as a diversity candidate.

"When you come out later in life, as I did, you find there's so much you can learn and teach," Norberg says. "I had many conversations with our CEO, who was African American, and because of *his* openness, we were able to do some things at McDonald's that we might not have done if we didn't have an open and honest interaction."

Being authentic with his CEO was a necessity.

"I wanted the leadership at McDonald's to know about my being gay before rumors started to fly," Norberg said. "The CEO, who always called me by my last name, said, 'Norberg, you have always been a great leader, but today you are even a better leader. You need to do for the LGBT community what I am trying to do for the African American community.'"

Coming out also revealed the CEO's humanity: Norberg learned that his colleague's brother-in-law had died of AIDS at the height of the epidemic.

Norberg has no problem with being chosen for a board directorship on the basis of his sexual orientation.

"Just like if you're looking for a CFO when you're going after a certain skill, your board would benefit from the value and diversity I bring to the table as a gay man."

Surely, I understand why some people are hesitant about viewing LGBTQ+ as a legitimate minority with a legitimate voice. They fear that boards will have to accommodate "personal preference" while compromising on qualifications, experience, and seniority.

I made the point many times in my January 2016 LinkedIn post: "Make no mistake, it is ALWAYS qualifications first and the BEST person for the job. However, wouldn't it be nice to open the boardroom doors to all types of people with differing perspectives and life experiences? In this way, deliberations and decision-making can be more robust and therefore more effective."[131]

* * *

The good—but not completely great—news is that some Fortune 500 companies have decent LGBTQ+ inclusion policies. The bad news is that inclusion has not yet reached the boardroom. Out Leadership recently reported the results of research into LGBTQ+ diversity on Fortune 500 boards. "Only five Fortune 500 companies have any LGBTQ+ policies within their proxy statements." Furthermore, "of the 5,670 board seats in the Fortune 500, only 25 seats (0.4 percent) are held by out LGBTQ+ people, and some of those seats are held by the same individuals."[132]

"When companies go to search firms, they say, 'Give us diverse candidates,'" says Paul Wendel, former manager of Talent Initiatives at Out Leadership. "They say, 'We want gender diversity. We want racial diversity.' But they haven't asked for sexual orientation diversity. For most companies, we believe, this is something that has been overlooked."[133] Companies are currently still trying to focus on visible diversity while LGBTQ+ identities may be invisible and thus more challenging to tackle, measure, and change.

Wendel told me that even the most forward-thinking US-based companies have not reviewed their diversity guidelines for twenty years.[134] That's a staggering thought when you think about the dramatic changes LGBTQ+ people have experienced since the 1990s, when President Bill Clinton came under attack for nominating openly gay James C. Hormel as ambassador to Luxembourg, when Senator Jesse Helms of North Carolina called gay people "degenerates," and when Senate Majority Leader Trent Lott of Mississippi referred to homosexuality as a pathology in need of treatment.[135] Fast-forward to 2018, when marriage between same-sex couples is legal in all fifty states (even while thirteen states have refused to comply with the Supreme Court's 2015 ruling that it is unconstitutional for states to ban same-sex marriages),[136] and when Supreme Court rulings between 2015 and 2017 have made adoption by gay couples legal.[137] And while some organizations are still using religious exemptions to discriminate against LGBTQ+ people, and legislative efforts are underway to deny transgender people equal protection under the law,[138] the time has come for companies to acknowledge the LGBTQ+ community as a unique category that deserves legal protection and corporate representation. As Wendel says, companies should update their guidelines to include LGBTQ+ as a significant—and necessary—board constituency.

Change is afoot, Wendel says. But there's just not enough of it.

"We have one search firm we work with that is committed to push for LGBTQ+ inclusion," he says. "They have asked us to give them a slate of diverse director candidates. But at the board level, most search firms aren't asking for LGBTQ+ candidates because the companies they work with aren't asking for them either."[139]

LGBTQ+ representation on boards may not come easily, but it is on the way.

NYC comptroller Scott Stringer's Board Accountability Project puts forth a board matrix[140] that lists "LGBTQ+" and "Non-Binary" as two distinct line-item categories.

The California Department of Insurance announced in 2014 a Governing Board Diversity (GBD) Survey, the first in the nation to examine the state of diversity—including board members who identify as LGBT—among insurer governing boards. According to the California DOI website, "It is meant to encourage insurance companies to seek a leadership and a board that is reflective of the changing demographics and diversity within California and the rest of the nation."[141] The survey requires that all companies with written premiums of $100 million or more in California report on the demographic composition of the board, leadership among its diverse board members, and outreach efforts and strategies to diversify board membership. That's progress, don't you think?

And of course, there is California's unprecedented boards diversity quota. Bill 979, signed into law in September 2020, states that corporations with principal offices in California "have at least one director from an 'underrepresented community'" on their board by the close of calendar year 2021, and it sets further targets for board membership by the close of the 2022 calendar year, depending on total board size. AB 979 defines a "director from an underrepresented community" as a director who self-identifies as "Black, African American, Hispanic, Latino, Asian, Pacific Islander, Native American, Native Hawaiian, or Alaska Native, or who self-identifies as gay, lesbian, bisexual, or transgender."[142] There is much debate about the constitutionality of this law, as well as the challenge of finding

The reality is that LGBTQ+ representation amounts to seventeen openly gay board directors across all Fortune 500 companies. That is 0.3 percent of all directors.

those whose diversity is not immediately obvious. Out Leadership and Quorum have a solution! They have built a database of more than nine hundred LGBTQ+ board-interested executives.

Like Paul Wendel, Stephanie Sandberg, former managing director of Out Leadership, cautions against an excess of optimism.

"If LGBTQ+ board representation is not happening at the level of culture, and if it's not happening at the highest corporate level, you're not really going to have much change,"[143] she told me.

Of course, Sandberg is right. The reality is that LGBTQ+ representation amounts to twenty-five openly gay board directors across all Fortune 500 companies. That is 0.4 percent of all directors.

But Sandberg has a solution. She believes CEOs can do more than almost anybody else to welcome and celebrate diversity—including LGBTQ+ diversity.

"You don't have to go around the table and say, 'Okay, who's gay here?' Just let it be known that all are welcome."[144]

That's not asking too much.

And by the way, even as this chapter is being written, this entire debate and discussion is on the verge of becoming obsolete. Remarkably, a 2016 survey by the consumer insight agency J. Walter Thompson Innovation Group found that only 48 percent of Generation Z identifies as "completely heterosexual."[145] Additionally, millennials are more than twice as likely (20 percent vs. 7 percent) to identify as LGBTQ+ than the boomer generation (people ages fifty-two to seventy-one) and two-thirds (20 percent vs. 12 percent) more likely than Generation X (people ages thirty-five to fifty-one).[146] This is reality. We are still discussing these constructs and business challenges in baby boomer terms, and reality has changed. In the not-too-distant future, Gen Z will assume leadership roles in our corporations and their boards. and whether we like it or not, the thinking is going to change.

CHAPTER 7

HISPANIC BOARD DIRECTORS: FEW AND FAR BETWEEN

Whether born from experience or inherent physiological or cultural differences, our gender and national origins may and will make a difference in our judging.

—SONIA SOTOMAYOR

The need for diversity on boards remains a well-rehearsed conversational refrain. So does the recognition that diversity of ideas and perspectives is critical for sound decision-making. And yet, as we've seen, the numbers are not where they need to be in terms of gender, racial, ethnic, and sexual orientation diversity.

Diversity of thought is key. And one way to get to diversity of thought is through diversity of ethnicity. Like other ethnic minorities, Hispanics have been largely underrepresented in boardrooms, and there is a multitude of good reasons for increasing their representation. Hispanics currently represent 18.1 percent of the US population. They are the largest and fastest-growing minority in the United States. In 2015, the Census Bureau projected that, by 2060, the Hispanic population will comprise 28.6 percent of the total population—about 119 million people.[147] In fact, the United States has a larger Spanish-speaking population than many Hispanic countries, including Peru and Venezuela.[148] More on this later in the chapter.

The Hispanic consumer is the fastest-growing segment of the US economy. The Latino community accounts for nearly half of all consumer spending growth in the United States.[149] Nationally, Hispanics represent $1.7 trillion in annual purchasing power. That's a significant increase from $21 billion in 1990 and just over $1 trillion as recently as 2010.[150] Hispanics outspend other groups in many categories, including grocery, clothing, and furniture purchases.[151] Strikingly, the National Association of Hispanic Real Estate Professionals (NAHREP) 2015 State of Hispanic Homeownership report shows that Hispanic households grew by 245,000. That is 69 percent of the total United States household growth. Additionally, another very interesting report from the Better Homes and Gardens Real Estate & NAHREP Hispanic Women Survey shows that the purchasing power and the primary decision makers in a Hispanic home are the women. A staggering 61 percent think they will make most of the decisions in their next home buying process.[152]

Again, Hispanic people hold the title of the largest minority in the United States, with only Mexico boasting a larger Hispanic population. Despite all this, Hispanics amount to just 3.8 percent of board members at Fortune 500 companies (4.4 percent when looking only at the Fortune 100).[153]

The numbers are even lower when it comes to Fortune 1000 companies, where Hispanic board members have remained at about 2.1 percent since 2015, with more than 82 percent of those companies having no Hispanic board members at all.[154] That said, there has been some progress on this front. During the two-year period from 2017 to 2019, there was a 14 percent increase in the number of board seats held by Hispanics.[155] Still minor but some progress, nonetheless.

As we see, most companies have no Hispanics in their board-rooms. This omission has pervasive ramifications, many of which go unrecognized. For example, companies miss critical insights serving a growing and significant customer base if no one from that base is contributing to decisions about the short- and longer-term direction of the company. We may realize what we are missing only once we find it and see the value and contributions in action.

In earlier chapters, we acknowledged some overlap among the obstacles faced by different minorities. For instance, the lack of board diversity is often attributed to a sparse supply of board-ready candidates from every minority category. There are presumably not enough women, Black people, Asian Americans, or Hispanics ready, willing, and qualified to enter our boardrooms. We also know that people tend to be more accepting of those who are similar to them. Ingroup favoritism has been studied and documented for decades by psychologists, anthropologists, and sociologists, among others. In fact, there is an evolutionary purpose for this human tendency which persists today: Our ancestors lived in small social groups that had frequent conflict with other groups over food, territory, and other limited resources. Other groups were seen as dangerous, and this served to keep each group separate and safe. Is it such a stretch to assume ingroup favoritism has survived until today?

* * *

Although we often cluster all board outsiders together, each group that is currently not well represented in boardrooms faces its own unique set of challenges. For example, Hispanics are the largest minority group in the United States: "statistics from 2017 show that Hispanics make up 17% of the work force but only represent 4.3%

of executive positions." The gap between the labor force and executive representation is currently wider among Hispanics than any other group.[156] In spite of this, I am regularly astounded by senior executives who check every board-director box, who are Hispanic, yet are not on boards and rarely even considered for opportunities.

Separately, Hispanic businesses are growing at fifteen times the rate of companies overall.[157] Hispanic entrepreneurs accounted for 86 percent of new business formation in the US since 2015.[158] These are primarily small- to midsized companies, but their founders, owners, and executives surely have experience and track records

The gap between the labor force and executive representation is currently wider among Hispanics than any other group.

that are applicable to other similar sized companies and their boards. Those boards should be looking to these individuals. Like their corporate brethren, they bring diversity, but perhaps more importantly, they bring experience with strategy, execution, financial management, and a systems-thinking expertise that will be helpful in the boardroom.

While we continue to grow the pipeline, companies that are interested in bringing Hispanic perspective to their boardroom can also look to former government officials and leaders. Highly regulated businesses would do particularly well with someone with this type of expertise. Furthermore, there is a wealth of talent within the ranks of the legal profession, as well as recently retired audit partners. As has been emphasized so often in this book, it is not a supply problem. We must be aware that many options exist, and simply relying on what has worked in the past is not the best way to make the progress that is necessary.

Part of the challenge some Hispanics face in reaching the boardroom is that they are not easily identified as such. Wait—before you turn the page in frustration, please be aware of the following reality. The value of diversity is still not fully understood by some corporations and their boards, even though they commit to making change and improvements. In these cases, where it is very much a compliance or public relations exercise, the company will want recognition that they have been a good corporate citizen and appointed a minority to their board. Thus, diversity needs to be perceptible. The truth is not all diversity is obvious, and this is where some of the challenge comes in. For example, years ago I was doing a board search for a large insurance company. They requested a Hispanic candidate for numerous reasons, including the fact that much of their business was in South America. Among the candidates we identified were several with a Hispanic mother and non-Hispanic father. These candidates were Hispanics in every way except they had surnames like Jones or Smith or some other non-Hispanic-sounding name. It turned out that this company didn't want to consider the candidates with non-Hispanic last names, because they believed the company wouldn't get the "credit" for having added a Hispanic to its board. Rather than appreciate the business case for diversity, they relegated it to a compliance exercise for which they expected credit in the public domain. Incidentally, I have experienced this on multiple occasions.

Finally, by definition, Hispanic refers to those from Spanish-speaking countries. Being a native Spanish speaker, or put another way, a nonnative English speaker, has many implications. The good news is that we know that language impacts one's view of the world. Our mother tongue molds the way we see the world, and boardrooms can benefit from this. The bad news is that there is a well-documented glass ceiling for nonnative speakers. According to a *Harvard Business*

Review study published in 2014 *"native speakers were, on average, 16% likelier to be recommended for"* managerial roles.[159] Wharton management professor Laura Huang found a widespread bias in the business community against nonnative English speakers. Entrepreneurs with nonnative accents, she noted, are significantly less likely to receive new-venture funding, and job candidates with nonnative accents are also less likely to be recommended for management positions. This paper was published in the *Journal of Applied Psychology*.[160] While not acceptable, this is surely understandable, as who among us has not made a snap judgment based on an accent. The problem is that we don't discuss these issues in the boardroom and are, for the most part, not even aware that they may be impacting our decision-making.

So again we must ask ourselves the million-dollar question, how can we change the situation? And the short answer is, it's complicated!

Part of the solution requires going back to education. As of right now, the long road to the C-suite and boardroom still typically begins with a college degree. This is true for most who are not the Bill Gateses and Mark Zuckerbergs of the world. An analysis of educational opportunities and impediments for Hispanics (and other minorities) merits a book of its own (and there are many). However, it is encouraging to note that according to the Pew Research Center, "about a quarter (26%) of recently arrived Latino immigrants ages twenty-five and older had a bachelor's degree or more education in 2018, up from just 10% in 1990."[161] Additionally, according to the US Department of Education, Hispanic undergraduate enrollment more than doubled from 2000 to 2015.[162]

This is good news on the education front, and hopefully this leads to changes in workforce opportunity. However, we must also be mindful that Hispanics in the workforce are not necessarily being endorsed by their employers in ways that help to prepare or mentor them for increased levels of responsibility. We must ask ourselves how corporations and other organizations can ensure that Hispanics who would like to be in the fast lane can get there and actually stay there. In other words, what sort of awareness and preparation might begin in an organization—with the newest employees in the most junior positions—to make sure that talented people make the sort of progress in their careers that allows them to reach the top?

Attention to previously mentioned unconscious biases combined with thoughtful mentoring of employees are ways to help make board candidate pools more robust. Another way is to make sure that Hispanic employees are considered for "developmental" positions— that is, positions that challenge them to grow and develop skills and expertise in areas that they have previously not been exposed to. This is a far cry from current practices, in which only 8 percent of managerial and 6 percent of professional positions in the US are filled by Hispanics.[163]

It has also been suggested that cities can contribute to nurturing Hispanic entrepreneurship and business participation by promoting educational opportunities at local universities, building business incubator programs, and supporting business development groups for Hispanics.[164]

We must also be aware of the problem of self-perpetuation. If you don't currently have a diverse board or C-suite, it may be more difficult to recruit diverse candidates. If prospective employees do not see themselves reflected at certain milestone points along the corporate ladder, in senior management, and/or the board they may be less likely to be interested in your organization. There is less to aspire to when the faces in those roles don't resemble their own. This, and the following suggestions, incidentally hold true for all underrepresented minorities.

Another solution is something we have discussed in earlier chapters. The very definition of "board ready" and "board qualified" must continue to evolve. Prior to the last decade or so, board directors were generally CEOs, CFOs, or recently retired CEOs and CFOs. A sitting CEO might find himself sitting on two or three outside boards at the same time, in addition to his own board and, of course, running his company ("his" is used intentionally here). This does not happen today. Overboarding is closely monitored and seriously frowned upon. In fact, "it has been determined and is becoming increasingly well known that corporations take on elevated risk when a director sits on an excessive number of boards."[165] As a result, chief marketing officers, chief information officers, chiefs of human resources, and chief digital officers have been welcomed into boardrooms in increasing numbers. In particular, technology's never-ending evolution has very recently opened the door even wider. Every board requires digital transformation, technology, cybersecurity, and the like. And if they don't, they should! These executives provide an excellent pool of board candidates who can make significant contributions, all the while bringing diversity to the table as well.

Large, publicly traded companies remain most cautious about who they put on their boards. The criteria are stringent with good reason. However, this is not an excuse for remaining homogeneous.

Part of the challenge of change resides in the fact that there are no universally accepted qualifications for board directors.

There are qualified directors at every level who are ready, willing, and able, and it is incumbent on these corporations or their trusted search partners to identify these people, properly assess them, and then assert whether they are qualified and belong on the board in question. Of course, this is more difficult than going for the tried and true. But ultimately inertia is not in the best interest of any company and its stakeholders.

Part of the challenge of change resides in the fact that there are no universally accepted qualifications for board directors, and importantly much is debated when it comes to what it means to be a successful director. In fact, it is only recently that evaluations of board members are even administered, and for the most part, the means of conducting these evaluations are still rudimentary. There are surveys and questionnaires, along with both self-evaluation and peer-evaluation, but the system of board evaluation is not as sophisticated as you might think. If anything, what we are learning so far from using these tools is that there are significant discrepancies in people's beliefs about what qualifies as adequate or successful board participation.

What's most interesting about the fledgling status of board evaluations is that at every other step of our careers, we are accustomed to regular evaluations of our performance. It starts with report cards in school and continues from there. But boardrooms have always been above and beyond these measures. I've consulted with senior executives in large public companies who've noticed that a particular director is not performing. But in the same breath, they'll acknowledge that it's unclear how to proceed in light of that recognition: "This director is clearly not performing and should be off the board. But we don't have any idea how to do that!" Part of the challenge is that there is frequently an unwillingness to have difficult conversations with under- or nonperforming board members. Board directors believe themselves to be more or less equal in stature, and there is an expectation of collegiality. Attempting to improve one another's behavior and performance is just too delicate a task for many boards.

It's true that we want and appreciate collegiality among board members and between boards and the companies they help serve. But too much collegiality—especially if there is an absence of clear performance criteria—often yields to situations in which everyone likes everyone else, and no one is fully objective. When relationships, harmony, and goodwill are too strong an objective, good judgment and independence of thought may be abandoned.

However, when it comes to board assessments, the cat is out of the bag. Since the financial crisis of 2008, we have got new legislation that has increased the pressure for boards to do their jobs well by holding them more accountable for the things that go on in the organizations they serve. Incredibly, it wasn't that long ago that some boards behaved more like a cool insiders' club and the capstone position of one's career rather than the arduous and serious responsibility that they truly are. Now more than ever before, the implications of sitting on a board are finally being appreciated. This means we need to better elucidate the definition of successful and effective board service and our ideas about acceptable board qualifications.

Recently the Latino Corporate Directors Association launched The Latino Board Tracker. This database allows for easy identification of those 75 percent of Fortune 1000 companies that lack a single Hispanic director.[166] As we know, what gets measured, gets managed. As of writing, of the top twenty-five companies on this list, only ten had a Hispanic person on their board. The smallest twenty-five of this list had a grand total of three Hispanics on their boards. If Hispanics are soon to become nearly a third of the population of the US, shouldn't their representation on boards be reflective of this?

In the end, the reason board diversity matters so much is that corporate sustenance is precarious, and all companies need the best possible tools and assets to succeed. Company boards must reflect company stakeholders. It is no longer sufficient to have an ivory tower full of individuals weighing in on matters in a detached and theoretical way. Our boards must speak from experience, from authentic understanding, and only then can we hope to be truly optimizing ourselves.

CHAPTER 8

WHAT MESSAGE ARE YOU SENDING YOUR EMPLOYEES?

It is not the strongest of the species that survive, nor the most intelligent, but the one most responsive to change.

—CHARLES DARWIN

The workplace and very nature of employment continues to change. Within the span of a few short weeks in March of 2020, we learned that companies do not need offices and people do not need physical proximity to work and make progress in their jobs. What else have we inaccurately assumed to be a best practice?

Millennials (born 1981 to 1996) and Generation Z (1997 to 2012) continue to make up more and more of the workforce, and companies need to understand the massive implications of this shifting demographic. According to a Pew Research Center analysis of US Census Bureau data, as of 2017 more than one in three American labor force participants (35 percent) are millennials, making them the largest generation in the US labor force.[167] Research and data projected that Gen Z would comprise about 36 percent of the workforce by 2020.[168] Although there are significant differences between these two demographics, for the sake of simplicity we are grouping them together because the main purpose here is to distinguish them from baby boomers (1946 to 1964) and the ensuing Gen X (1965 to 1980). Baby boomers and Gen X currently make up the bulk of the boardroom and corner offices, but every day they are reaching retirement age in droves.

Millennial and Gen Z employees have a unique view of work and careers and very different priorities than generations that have come before them. To attract them as employees, investors, suppliers, or customers, it is necessary to understand what makes them tick.

Millennials and Generation Z, for example, tend not to distinguish between work hours and home hours in the same way that we have for generations. As digital natives, they work from anywhere and at any time. The traditional nine-to-five workday has gone the way of the fax machine.

Changing employers is also no longer a once or twice in a lifetime event. In fact, a recent study reveals that 21 percent of millennials say they've changed jobs within the past year, which is more than three times the number of nonmillennials who report the same.[169] Gold watches for thirty years of service at retirement parties are also a thing of the past.

Purposeful work and social impact are no longer optional.

These younger employees are far more discerning about the companies they work for than ever before. The values and culture of the organization figure prominently in decision-making and loyalty. In fact, 43 percent of Gen Z employees say that a company's mission, purpose, and values play a huge role in determining how long they'll stay in a given position. Millennials and Gen Z also have high expectations for the actions of companies when it comes to social purpose and accountability; and they want to work for companies that uphold these values. Purposeful work and social impact are no longer optional.

There may have been elements of this in past generations, but what is markedly different now is that employees are not afraid to voice their opinions and lobby for change. So-called employee activism has been rising, and companies would be well advised to pay attention. For example, in 2019, Amazon experienced employees walking out of work to protest the company's environmental impact. Furniture retailer Wayfair experienced employee protests as a response to the company selling furniture to detention centers that housed migrant children. Google, Microsoft, and Apple are some of the other companies that have experienced employee activism and the consequent requests to justify themselves and various business decisions they made.

Employee activism does not only concern one-off business choices but can be used to pressure and put a magnifying glass on leadership as well. Again, Amazon provides a case in point when its employees demanded greater boardroom diversity.

The company fracas began after CtW Investment Group, which works with union-sponsored pension funds that have more than $250 billion in assets, called upon Amazon in late 2017 to increase gender diversity among its executive ranks and corporate board.[170] CtW executive director Dieter Waizenegger argued in a letter to then Amazon CEO Jeff Bezos that the alleged harassment by Amazon Studios president Roy Price of an Amazon studio producer "stems ultimately from Amazon's failure to ensure that women have the opportunity to rise to the highest ranks within Amazon's workforce."

Waizenegger asked further that Amazon "implement a 'Rooney Rule' requiring that the initial list of candidates from which new director nominees are chosen should include (but need not be limited to) qualified women and minority candidates."[171]

A reminder about the Rooney Rule, named for former Pittsburgh Steelers owner Dan Rooney: It came about in 2003 to address the under recruitment of minority coaches in professional football, who, despite their successes, were not being considered for high-level coaching positions.[172] The rule requires National Football League teams to interview ethnic-minority candidates for head coaching and senior football operation jobs. The Rooney Rule now refers to minority recruitment initiatives across all industries.

Amazon bristled at CtW's perceived intervention in its board recruitment. Amazon issued a statement that promised a commitment to diversity and inclusion but maintained that the "Rooney Rule is not the right approach at this time."[173]

Amazon's employees bristled right back at a communications executive who attempted to justify the corporate response.

"What exactly is the complex process that we currently use to find and vet talent that we are so proud of?" one employee asked in an email thread reviewed by Recode, a technology news website.[174]

"How is it successful, if we aren't diverse at all, and notably last amongst top tech companies?" the same employee continued. "Please provide your measures for success."

The employee ended her response with a call to action:

"We have a chance to be the FIRST to tackle this amongst top tech companies, but whenever diversity issues come up, we run from data and sprint towards overelaboration and buzzwords… I know there are many people internally working hard on [diversity] issues… We don't need more effort, we need COURAGE."

Another Amazon employee concluded, "Does anyone else see the possible bias that could result with a board made up of predominately older white males (the youngest person on the Board is Bezos himself) unilaterally making this decision on race and gender diversity?"

Was employee outrage worth it?

Well, it got attention far beyond the Amazon campus. The House Tech Accountability Caucus and the Congressional Black Caucus, which ultimately acknowledged Bezos for finally doing the right thing, said in a joint statement: "American companies' boardrooms, executive suites, and sales floors should aspire to be representative of the customers they serve."[175]

Precisely the point.

Of course, no one is suggesting that companies yield to all demands, but the immense disruption, bad press, and ensuing turbulence should be reason enough to pay attention. Employees of the past may or may not have objected to the lack of diversity within their own companies. If they did, it was generally with job dissatisfaction and all the consequences this entails, or perhaps they left their employer. Although this has enormous costs and consequences to organizations, they were largely immeasurable. Today's employees may no longer want to acquiesce.

To remain competitive, companies must pay attention to this changing workforce. Attitudes toward and evidence of diversity are changing, as is the mere nature and interpretation of diversity. Religious and political beliefs, as well as culture and even disability and veteran status, are now taken into consideration when discussing the topic of diversity. Yes, it is complex, and it is expected to get even more so.

Many companies have yielded to the grassroots call for greater diversity by implementing various initiatives. These may include recruiting diverse employees, trainings on inclusion and unconscious bias, and perhaps celebrating holidays and events of different minority groups. Most of these approaches have not changed much since they began in the 1960s. And all too often these programs and efforts have limited value because employees look at the senior executive team and the board of directors and see the same old same old. Diversity initiatives must include the very top of the organization. A diversity initiative that begins and ends in the middle of an organization is likely to be perceived as nothing more than a compliance exercise or part of a marketing program. Consequently, it will likely generate cynicism and even resistance among employees.

When they do not begin at the top, what do employees ultimately conclude about diversity initiatives?

When they do not begin at the top, what do employees ultimately conclude about diversity initiatives? No matter what the company says, and despite the training and other programs, there is really no room at the top for women and minorities. How seriously do employees take diversity messaging when the top brass talks the talk but doesn't walk the walk? You do not want your employees to think your diversity initiatives are corporate propaganda!

* * *

Accenture has reported that "there is a large gap between what leaders think is going on and what employees say is happening on the ground. Two thirds of leaders (68 percent) feel they create empowering environments—in which employees can be themselves, raise concerns, and innovate without fear of failure—but just one third (36 percent) of employees agree." This research also found the proportion of employees who do not feel included in their organizations (i.e., who do not feel they are welcome at work and can contribute fully and thrive) is 20 percent, which is ten times higher than leaders believe (2 percent).[176] Lest you gloss over this as fluff, in this same research,

Accenture suggests that if the employee perception gap were reduced by 50 percent, global profits are estimated to increase by 33 percent for a global total of $3.7 trillion on 2019.

That is $3.7 trillion!

For improvement to occur, employees need to recognize that there is no glass ceiling, that the company values hard work and talent in all their employees, regardless of race, gender, or sexual orientation. The best way to achieve this is to begin with a boardroom and corner office that are reflective of these values. Let's stop talking about it and preparing for it and simply do it.

* * *

London-based change-management consultant Sylvia Storey told the *Financial Times* that companies may publicize one-off diversity initiatives but few are "able to marry their financial outcomes (ROI) with their diversity initiatives, because there are no measures or lines of accountability in place at the top."[177] She told the UK newspaper further that diversity and inclusion initiatives can only make inroads "where the leader of the organization has championed it and formed councils, board positions, and [performance measures] to amplify and demonstrate his/her commitment to the cause."

Storey's recommendation makes a lot of sense because actions speak louder than words. But change does not come without major challenges and even some resistance. One study found that White male employees—"members of high-status groups"—may respond negatively to companies that promote diversity "because they see efforts to foster diversity as coming at the expense of individuals such as themselves."[178] To illustrate, Google discovered in August 2017 that its diversity initiatives were met with hostility by James Damore, a then twenty-eight-year-old software engineer, who disseminated a ten-page memo, in which he viewed such initiatives as "discrimination to reach equal representation," and that this discrimination was "unfair, divisive, and bad for business."[179] But Google, now Alphabet, which has three women on its board (27 percent), took honorable action. It fired Damore on grounds that he violated company rules by "advancing harmful gender stereotypes."[180]

For some members of "high-status groups," any sign of diversity in the workplace, the C-suite, or the corporate board is a personal threat. Kudos to Google for sending a message to employees that it will nip sexual, gender, ethnic, and racial harassment in the bud because it is bad—not just for business but also for employee esprit de corps. Google's commitment to diversity stands in stark contrast to the 457 companies in the Russell 3000 whose boards were still 100 percent male at the end of 2018[181] and the more than 82 percent of Fortune 1000 companies that still have no Hispanic board members.

It also stands in stark contrast to Uber, which mishandled the sexual harassment of various female engineers by a male manager in 2016. During CEO Travis Kalanick's tenure, the manager was allowed to retain his position while the women were "encouraged" to look for other work arrangements inside the company. "There was nothing any of us could do," wrote former Uber engineer Susan Fowler. "We all gave up on Uber HR and our managers after that. Eventually [that manager] 'left' the company. I don't know what he did that finally convinced them to fire him."[182]

Uber had only one woman on its board during Fowler's employment. That was HuffPost founder Arianna Huffington, who incited a firestorm during an investigation of Uber by then US Attorney General Eric Holder when she said that sexual harassment was not a systemic issue at the company.[183]

Today Uber has four women on its board, representing 40 percent of the board seats. The executive team is 30 percent women and 50–60 percent ethnically diverse, depending on the diversity definition employed. This is enormous progress and demonstrates what is possible.

* * *

A company without female or minority board representation, or with token representation, sends out several messages that employees take to heart:

- We are a company that does not care whether employees see themselves represented at the highest corporate level.

- We are a company that may not acknowledge sexism—in the workplace, in the boardroom.

- We are a company that prefers homogeneity because we don't want "outsiders" on "our" board.

The lasting message:

Diversity is just a compliance exercise. In the C-suite and the boardroom where the company is run, nothing much has really changed.

* * *

What do millennial and Gen Z employees think when they look at the board of directors and the top of the organizational chart and do not see themselves reflected there? What do they conclude when they see forty-four directors of US public companies who are ninety years old and older? Or 764 directors who are more than eighty years old. These men (738 are men) were brilliant executives for decades, but it's entirely possible that they exceeded their shelf life as our economy has moved from analog to digital technologies and artificial intelligence has moved beyond science fiction movies.

How else to explain the belief of Les Wexner, founder of L Brands, that the "internet won't kill stores" and the "fascination with smartphones will fade."[184] Wexner made this observation in February 2018, just months after fifty retailers filed for bankruptcy, including Gymboree Corp., Payless ShoeSource, and Toys 'R' Us. L Brands itself has suffered the same fate as other real-world retailers with sagging same-store sales and a share price that fell 50 percent since late 2015. This is not to say that we no longer need seniors on boards. Rather, most boards would do better if not entirely made up of one generation.

When corporate boards are stacked with people who do not acknowledge and understand the impact and importance that employees—with their sensitivity to social, consumer, and technology trends—have on a company, corporate profits and shareholder value are likely to take a hit. All of us have witnessed the rise and fall of decades-old companies; eventually, the climate becomes ripe for interlopers who are tuned in to new business models and customer preferences.

Google employees also rose to the occasion nearly a year after James Damore distributed his antidiversity memo. At the June 2018 annual shareholder meeting at Google parent company Alphabet, employees challenged executive and board management on diversity issues. One female engineer insisted that Alphabet tie executive pay to improving diversity metrics.[185]

Google shareholders rejected the proposal.

Yet employee voices at Google continue to be heard. Some four thousand Google workers reportedly signed a petition demanding that the company cancel a Department of Defense initiative aimed at developing better artificial intelligence for the US military. In late

May 2018 Google canceled the DoD contract and agreed not to pursue similar ones.

Someday Alphabet management may heed that previously mentioned female engineer's voice too.

You may find it convenient to resist all the grassroots groups agitating for more diverse board representation. But your employees take their cues from corporate decisions that affect their careers, opportunities, and aspirations. Are they being forced to go through diversity training exercises that only leave them disgruntled and cynical? Do they believe, as many employees did in decades past, that employees could be seen but not heard?

Employees, especially the millions of millennials and Gen Zs joining the workforce, feel increasingly empowered to speak out on their own behalf. They are not holding back from expressing their dissatisfaction with company leadership. And that includes the board of directors.

To be sure, diverse representation at the top of any organization is not the end in and of itself. The theory is that change starts at the top. Culture starts at the top. To truly embrace diversity is to let actions speak louder than words. Create a diverse board and embrace all the value that this brings with it. Be authentic in this, and the trickle-down effect will be more than worth the effort.

For any business or organization, employees are its most valuable resource. Exceptional talent can take a good business and make it great and even take a failing enterprise and turn it around. Employees want to know: Is there room at the top for me—or does diversity really just mean business as usual?

CHAPTER 9

IS THAT BOARD MEMBER NAPPING, OR DID HE JUST PASS AWAY?

I know there is strength in the differences between us. I know there is comfort, where we overlap.

—ANI DIFRANCO

The title of this chapter means no disrespect. There is great value in the wisdom that can come only through experience. All boards need this. However, they do not need only this. There is extreme value in age diversity, and this is the message I hope to convey.

Domenico Dolce and Stefano Gabbana, owners of the Dolce & Gabbana fashion label, seat young YouTube and Instagram personalities at their shows and hire celebrities' teenage children to walk the runways.[186] As fifty- and sixty-somethings, they know they must go outside their own age group to stay commercially relevant for their single most important stratum of consumers: young people.

"I saw that the young generation used the Internet like a private club," Dolce says. "They love sharing their private lives and experiences between them via social media. They know each other even if they live on the other side of the world … [Gabbana] and I thought maybe this is the moment we need to step into the next generation."

In April 2018, the cofounders opened a "luxe clubhouse"[187] in downtown Manhattan focused on millennials. The unisex attire includes painted leather goods, sneakers, and ready-to-wear pieces decorated with speeding yellow cabs and other iconic New York City images.[188] Rivals such as Burberry, whose stock price tanked nearly 8 percent in April 2017 after news of a slowdown in US and Hong Kong sales,[189] continue to struggle with a revenue decline of 6.25 percent between 2019 and 2020 while Dolce & Gabbana's revenue has "a healthy bounce in its step."[190]

Stock prices rise and fall for all kinds of reasons, but an inability to understand customer tastes never bodes well for shareholder value. If Dolce & Gabbana were still taking its inspiration from mid-1980s fashion trends and the disco era in which they met, how relevant would it be today, thirty-five years after its founding?

Dolce and Gabbana figured out how to sustain their company as a youth-minded fashion brand because they are what songwriters Carolyn Leigh and Johnny Richards called "young at heart." But what about the all-too-many apparel, tech, media, and other companies whose board members and C-suite executives are in their seventies, eighties, and even nineties?

In the last chapter we mentioned that at the time of writing, 44 directors of US public companies are ninety years old and older and 764 directors are more than eighty years old. In the UK there are 2 directors who are ninety and above and 59 who are eighty and above. In Canada there are 6 and 168. Granted, the UK and Canada have fewer directors of publicly traded companies, but no matter the country, there are well-established physical and cognitive changes associated with aging. Of course, not all people age in the same way, but regardless, wouldn't companies benefit from more regular refreshment of their boards? And even more importantly, shouldn't our society and business community encourage healthy retirement years? Indeed, many countries have a retirement age under sixty-five. In Canada, an individual can begin receiving some reduced pension as early as a month after their sixtieth birthday. In South Korea and Turkey, sixty years old is the age of retirement.[191] Yes, retirement is a very personal choice, but we do take our cues and preferences from the culture in which we live. I recall a visit to a mountain village in the northwest part of the Yunnan province in China. There I met several monks and lamas from the local and renowned Tibetan Monastery. They were very clear that in their early to midfifties, they were very much retired. They considered themselves old and looked forward to enjoying their retirement years. Yes, this is a different world, far from our own, both physically and culturally. The point is that our norms and standards are ours and not the only option. Many will disagree with the notion of retiring, but most also chuckle when they hear the oft repeated phase "on their deathbed no one will say they regret not having spent more time at the office."

As mentioned earlier, until recently L Brands' board of directors consisted almost entirely of men in their seventies and eighties[192]— and the companies' various holdings have been falling behind due to competitive pressure. For all its glory, Berkshire Hathaway may be the oldest board in the United States. The average age on this board is almost seventy-four years old, and there are four directors who are more than ninety years old. There are many such examples. In fact, viewing previously mentioned statistics in a different way, it may surprise some to know that in the US there are currently 456 directors on public-company boards who are eighty-five years of age and above. Will superaged boards and superaged directors contribute to the eventual eclipse of great companies?

Aging boards are ubiquitous. Some 80 percent of S&P 500 boards in every industrial sector have an average age in the sixties.[193] Sixty-somethings can be at the top of their game when it comes to expertise and experience. What's problematic is that more board members (558 of them) are older than seventy-five than under fifty (315).[194] Just 6 percent of S&P 500 directors are fifty or younger, and most of those are between forty-five and fifty.[195]

Recommendation via social media is the metric of the moment.

I am not making an argument in favor of ageism. That's why I began by talking about Dolce and Gabbana. They are not that young anymore, but they are tuned in. By contrast, the seventy- and eighty-year-olds sitting on boards today grew up well before the social-media age, even before the advent of the internet in some cases. And these technologies are so integral to the way millennials and Gen Z communicate and experience the world. To wit, hotel giant Marriott tracks what they say on Facebook, TikTok, and other social-media utilities about its "food and beverage incubator," a partnership between Marriott and local entrepreneurs around the world.[196] Recommendation via social media is the metric of the moment. The traditional metric on the margin that venues produce has become less significant for Marriott.[197] The takeaway: especially when it comes to consumer products and services, to survive we must overturn antiquated business thinking and practice. If you want to connect with a younger demographic, you must disengage from established assumptions and practices.

A great example of this is Starbucks. In 2011 Starbucks appointed Clara Shih to its board. "Clara is a true technology leader and will bring fresh insight to our strong and forward-thinking Board," said Howard Schultz, chairman, president, and CEO of Starbucks. "We could not be more thrilled about the social-media expertise and ideas Clara will bring to our business as we continue to amplify the online experience and interactions Starbucks has with our customers, partners and communities." At the time, Clara was twenty-nine. To be completely honest, at the time I scratched my head in wonder. Today, she is still on the board, and there are now seventy-three directors of US public companies who are thirty years old or younger.

Boards and the companies they serve must consider a balance between wisdom and the associated institutional knowledge and, on the other side, new ideas and experiences. Boards must proactively, consciously, and regularly assess this balance.

We cannot talk about older board members without considering the culture that shaped them. I remember some directors early in the internet era who did not know how to use the online portal that contained background materials for upcoming board meetings. Again and again, I would hear, "John doesn't know how to use the portal." Someone would have to get these materials printed out and shipped overnight to technologically challenged John. I hear this sort of thing still goes on today.

We shouldn't assume that every eighty-something board member will suffer from the antiquated perspective of board chairman and CEO Leslie Wexner, who—despite L Brands' flagging sales—contends the mall is the marketplace of the future. But what if an eighty-year-old director's last CEO position was in 1998? That's the year Google came into existence. Wikipedia followed in 2001, Facebook in 2004, YouTube in 2005, Twitter in 2006, iPhone and Kindle in 2007.[198] Instagram[199] and Pinterest,[200] sites with hundreds of millions of users, were both launched in 2010. Technological change in our social and business worlds is happening so fast that if you don't try to keep up, you are a technology dinosaur.

"There is a half-life for every board member," the *Financial Times* wrote in 2010, when discussing the issue of aging board directors. "Half-life is not based on the energy of the individual, but how long it's been since they've been in the game."[201]

When the marketplace speaks, can older board members (and CEOs) listen? A recent spate of executives in the packaged food and beverage industry have had to step down after their companies—including Campbell Soup Co., General Mills, Inc., Mondelez International, Inc., Kellogg Co., Nestle USA, Hershey Co., J.M. Smucker Co., and Hostess—reported consecutive quarters of profit declines. Many of their directors are in their sixties. Boards and executives have wrestled with a "new era of American eating and grocery shopping habits, shepherded in by millennials and the internet,"[202] according to *The Wall Street Journal.* Directors and C-level executives sincerely try to invest in change, yet the S&P 500 Packaged Food & Meat subindex has dropped 15 percent in the past two years, while the S&P 500 overall has climbed 30 percent.[203]

Hershey's chief digital commerce officer said the packaged foods industry for decades trained people to focus on physical stores, not e-commerce. "It's really hard to burst out of that mindset," he told the *Journal.*[204]

Bursting out of that mindset is exactly what MassMutual did when it set out to reach millennials. The financial services company stopped overtly selling products to this target audience, because millennials notoriously hate the hard sell. Instead, the company opened a high-tech/high-touch storefront in Brookline, Massachusetts, called Society of Grownups. The WeWork-style clubhouse includes a coffee bar, conference table, and meeting rooms where millennials can take financial literacy classes—as well as classes on travel and wine.[205] Many classes are sold out.

Asking boards to reserve seats for younger directors has nothing to do with ageism. It has to do with keeping boards relevant, current, and ever evolving.

If you do not keep up with the impact of technology on consumer habits and preferences—especially among young consumers—you will be obsolete.

Many Fortune 500 companies have international operations in markets dominated by young people. In 2012, about 66 percent of the population of the Middle East and Africa was under thirty, compared with 52 percent in Latin America and 48 percent in Asia.[206] As these markets continue to expand, isn't it good business practice to select board members who really understand their vast pools of consumers?

Another potential issue with older directors who are otherwise retired: when directorships are their only source of income, they can become financially dependent on their director compensation. A friend of mine was the chief operating officer in a publicly traded shoe company when he told me, "My board is filled with old men who need the money, and therefore they say yes to everything I propose."

Asking boards to reserve seats for younger directors has nothing to do with ageism. It has to do with keeping boards relevant, current, and ever evolving. It has to do with a board's ability to understand a business environment that changes by the nanosecond for every one of us. The best boards will be diverse in terms of age composition. Different generations, each providing value and unique insights.

Moreover, if people stay on a board forever, they are preventing other kinds of qualified directors, notably younger people, from joining. For a board to function optimally, older directors need to understand that the good of the company comes before their own purse and their own pastime. Former chairman and CEO of General Electric Jack Welch was famous for saying, "From now on, choosing my successor is the most important decision I'll make. It occupies a considerable amount of thought almost every day."[207] Welch reportedly made this assertion nine years before his anticipated retirement because he knew that one day relatively soon, for the good of the company, for the good of his shareholders, he would have to step aside. This thinking is applicable to the boardroom as well.

Think about athletes who leave at the top of their game. NBA star David Robinson exited basketball in 2003 at age thirty-eight after winning his second world championship.[208] The same exit strategy was true for thirty-four-year-old NASCAR driver Ned Jarrett, thirty-seven-year-old Joe DiMaggio, and thirty-two-year-old Rocky Marciano.[209] Many of these greats went on to have successful second careers. Robinson helped found Admiral Capital Group.[210] Jarrett took a Dale Carnegie course and found the courage to become a radio broadcaster.[211] DiMaggio became an advertising spokesman.[212] Marciano went on to a career as a TV sports commentator.[213] The cachet associated with leaving while you are still on top is huge.

Certainly, one eighty-something board member on a board of seven or eight companies might provide some wisdom and institutional knowledge. That elder may be equipped to understand the opportunities and challenges faced by firms and leverage their knowledge and network to advise the management team on important strategic decisions.[214] Older people can tap into their years of experience to provide unique insights. They may have seen the business or industry they are in evolve over time, and this historical perspective can be invaluable.

Additionally, certain businesses and industries simply lend themselves to a majority of older directors. For example, the board of an assisted living business can benefit enormously from having an older director (or several). Many other industries, indeed, may benefit from having some older directors. However, all boards should be composed of directors of different generations.

Along with aged directors can come long tenure. Serving on a board for over a decade can simply be too long. The specific number of years is currently under debate, but suffice it to say that, in governance circles, experts are currently discussing appropriate tenures of between nine and twelve years. It is believed that after this time one loses independence because one fall's prey to what sociologists call "co-optation." Over time, you have become more committed to preserving the stability of the organization, more concerned about managing opposition, and less engaged in strategic thinking. You also naturally develop bonds and relationships not only with other board members but with executives employed by the company. This will make independence and objectivity increasingly questionable.

An eighty-year-old today was over thirty in 1968. He was already a full-fledged adult during the Vietnam War and when Martin Luther King was shot dead. Imagine the robustness of a conversation between these individuals and those born at the end of the last century. The wildly different perspectives and experiences will most certainly yield better strategies, decisions, and perspectives.

In the words of Charles Darwin, "It is not the strongest of the species that survives, nor the most intelligent, but the ones most responsive to change."

CHAPTER 10

HERE COMES THE PRESSURE, AND IT'S NOT LETTING UP

Not everything that is faced can be changed, but nothing can be changed until it is faced.

—JAMES BALDWIN

When it comes to matters of parity and diversity in the corporate boardroom, no topic is more likely to generate debate than quotas. There's legitimate reason for the controversy. In the nineteenth and twentieth centuries, quotas in the US were designed to keep ethnic and racial minorities out of the mainstream. Yale University, for example, was unequivocal in its disdain for non-Whites and non-Protestants: "Never admit more than five Jews, take only two Italian Catholics, and take no blacks at all,"[215] Dean Milton Winternitz reportedly advised Yale's admissions team. During his tenure in the early 1900s, Harvard president Abbott Lawrence Lowell cautioned his admissions team against lifting a 15 percent cap on Jewish enrollment because too many Jews might incite "anti-Semitic feeling among the students."[216] In recent times, a coalition of Asian American groups filed a complaint with the US Justice and Education Departments alleging that Harvard and other universities use racial quotas to admit students other than high-scoring Asians.[217]

Other quotas have had life-and-death consequences. The Immigration Act of 1924,[218] a piece of omnibus legislation, set quotas on the number of immigrants from certain "undesirable" countries and enforced a ban on non-White immigrants. A law that seemed reasonable to the sixty-eighth US Congress had serious ramifications a few years down the road for millions of would-be emigrants trapped inside the Nazi empire.

Admittedly, quotas are a serious business. Like a toggle switch—a single button designed to close off or activate a circuit—a quota can close off an opportunity for one group or activate it for another. In the case of corporate boards, quotas reserving seats for women has become one way to compel companies to do, by mandate, what they were unwilling or unable to do voluntarily: give women a seat at the table. More recently we have begun to see quotas and mandates for ethnic, racial, and other types of diversity, as well.

Some countries have concluded that quotas are the fastest and surest way to female representation on corporate boards.

In 2003,[219] Norway became the first country to institute a quota to reserve at least 40 percent of board directorships at public companies for women.[220] This quota was meant to redress the gender imbalance typical of Norwegian boards, where women held 4 percent of all seats. Public companies were given until 2005 to achieve the target voluntarily. But by the deadline, women occupied only 18 percent of board seats. New legislation in 2006 required that all public companies achieve the 40 percent quota by 2008 or face financial penalties and, possibly, liquidation. Only 5 percent of companies failed to meet the requirement. Full compliance was in effect by 2009.[221] By 2015, women occupied 41 percent of board seats and 35 percent of boards of the twenty-five most traded companies listed on the Oslo Stock Exchange.[222] As of 2019 women comprised 42.5 percent of publicly listed company board seats in Norway. Compare this to the United States where the number is 23.5 percent for the entire Russell 3000.[223]

Other European countries have also passed quota legislation. Belgium, France, and Italy enacted binding quotas with sanctions for noncompliance almost a decade ago. Austria's quota came in 2018. The Netherlands and Spain do not have quotas but make recommendations. Finland and Greece established quotas for state-owned companies. And in March 2015, Germany passed legislation requiring a minimum of 30 percent of each gender on the boards of its largest listed companies.

Outside Europe, Malaysia instituted a 30 percent quota in 2013[224] for women on boards, with a target date of 2016. Brazil has gone with a 40 percent goal for state-owned companies.[225] India's Companies Act (2013) mandates that all listed companies have at least one woman on their board. Ireland, Israel, and Kenya have established quotas for state-owned companies.[226] The province of Quebec in Canada, which has a "comply or explain" approach much like the UK, requires gender parity on the boards of its Crown corporations.[227]

Until recently, the US, the UK, Canada, and Australia chose not to embrace mandatory quotas, opting instead to increase the number of women directors through voluntary initiatives and corporate disclosure requirements.[228] As cultural and political imperatives have evolved, though, some of these countries are moving away from voluntary targets to gender quotas. Australia's ASX Corporate Governance Council, for example, proposed in May 2018 that 30 percent of boardrooms be filled with women.[229]

In the US to date, the Securities and Exchange Commission (SEC) takes a less stringent view of gender inclusiveness, asking only that public companies disclose whether they consider diversity a factor in selecting board members. If the company has a diversity policy, it must disclose how it is implemented and how effective it is. The SEC permits individual companies to interpret what "diversity" means to them.[230]

In Canada, securities regulators in several provinces have published gender diversity disclosure obligations. Public companies must disclose whether they have a written policy for identifying women directors and whether they have percentage targets for boards and executive positions. One Canadian public action council has advocated for 30 percent female representation on boards but endorses the comply-or-explain approach that lets companies explain why they have chosen not to comply with boardroom diversity targets. Australia signed on to comply-or-explain in 2010.[231]

UK companies, which have endorsed disclosure requirements since 2006, are required every year to specify the number of directors by sex and to publish board policy on diversity, "including gender."[232] While sidestepping quotas, the UK government set up a commission in 2010 to identify the barriers that prevent women from reaching the boardroom—and to outline strategies to increase the proportion of women on corporate boards. Named for commission chairman Lord Davies of Abersoch, the Davies Review recommended that the Financial Times Stock Exchange (FTSE) 100 companies aim for a minimum of 25 percent female representation by 2015 and 30 percent by 2020.[233] The Davies Review, which ran from 2011 to 2015, increased the proportion of women serving on FTSE 100 boards from 12 percent to 25 percent. For FTSE 250 firms, it increased the proportion of women serving on boards from 9 percent to 22 percent. Subsequent to the Davies Review came the Hampton-Alexander Review which purports to continue the diversity work. The Hampton-

Alexander Review is working toward female board representation of 33 percent on FTSE350 boards by 2020. They also aim for 33 percent female representation on leadership teams by 2020.[234] This, of course, aims to create more of a pipeline of board candidates.

After years of objections about quotas, the climate in the US is changing. In September of 2018 California Governor Jerry Brown signed legislation (SB 826) stating that all publicly traded companies headquartered in California must have at least one woman on their board by the end of 2019 and two by the end of 2021. This was a game changer. This was also met by much resistance. There was talk about companies relocating headquarters out of California, as well as whether it is constitutional to mandate one group's inclusion over others. In August of 2019, the first lawsuit challenging this legislation was filed. In *Crest v. Alex Padilla*, it was alleged that SB 826 focused on an unconstitutional gender quota and also violates the California constitution.[235]

In August of 2019, the state of Illinois passed its own legislation, even more comprehensive than California's. This new legislation mandates that all publicly traded companies headquartered in Illinois must have not only gender diversity but racial and ethnic diversity on their boards by the end of 2020. Many lauded this legislation as more appropriate and equitable than the original in California.

So we see a broadening of the legislation on board diversity. In the United States no longer are we simply focused on gender diversity in the boardroom, but we have moved toward ethnic and racial diversity and even diversity of sexual orientation. The challenge associated with these latter diversity requirements is that they can be complicated to measure. There is a self-disclosure element that will be necessary in order to accurately gauge the current situation and measure progress.

Other states, including Massachusetts, Pennsylvania, and Colorado, have also passed nonbinding resolutions encouraging increased board diversity.[236]

All of this leads to the question: What is the preferred path to improved diversity? Quotas? Incentives? Spontaneity? The short answer is that it depends on who you ask.

In the US, where—other than recently in California—legal quotas for boardroom diversity have not existed, women and minorities occupy fewer seats than their counterparts in Norway, where quotas are compulsory. A 2016 Alliance for Board Diversity-Deloitte study[237] of Fortune 100 companies revealed that:

- Caucasian women occupied 221 seats (18.3 percent of all seats).

- Minority women occupied 56 seats (4.7 percent of all seats).

- Minority men occupied 155 seats (12.9 percent of all seats).

- Caucasian men occupied 773 seats (64.1 percent of all seats).[238]

It's painful to consider the reality: without quotas or Davies Review–style advocacy, gender diversity on US-based boards (23 percent)[239] is dramatically lower than gender diversity on Norwegian boards (46.7 percent)[240] and somewhat lower than gender diversity on UK-based boards (26.8 percent).[241]

We would not need quotas if, rather than thinking that diversity is some social exercise, we appreciated the true and comprehensive value that it can bring to an organization.

The Alliance for Board Diversity, which began conducting its census of Fortune 100 board directors in 2004, reported that gains for women and minorities in 2016 were "minimal."[242] Without some incentive or push, boards may procrastinate indefinitely. Personally, I have repeatedly heard the pushback: "We know, but we have a business to run and will get to it when we can." Implicit here is the sentiment that diversity is outside the core of running a business. We would not need quotas if, rather than thinking that diversity is some social exercise, we appreciated the true and comprehensive value that it can bring to an organization.

Until recently, cultural and political sentiment indicated that quotas would come at too great a cost in the US. Yet in the face of corporate resistance to diversity improvements, pressure from grassroots organizations for quotas—or targets—continues to mount. Previously mentioned, Senate Bill 826 passed in California mandated that corporations have at least one woman on their boards by the end of 2019. By 2021, boards with five members will need to have at least two women, and boards with six or more members will need at least three. Companies that do not comply may be fined $100,000 for the first violation and $300,000 for additional violations.[243]

Meanwhile, the Massachusetts House of Representatives unanimously voted in October 2015 to pass Resolution S1007 urging companies to put at least three women on their boards of nine or more directors by the end of 2018. Smaller companies would be expected to include at least two women.[244]

As the UK's *Guardian* newspaper put it, women "can't just ask politely"[245] anymore.

* * *

Institutional investors and grassroot efforts are also playing a significant role in the path forward.

The New York State Common Retirement Fund announced a campaign in early 2018 to oppose the reelection of all directors on

US corporate boards without at least one woman.[246] At the time of the fund's announcement, forty-five companies in the Russell 1500 index had not had a single female board member since 2006. The pension fund already has opposed, or plans on opposing, directors up for reelection at TransDigm Group, Inc., Seaboard Corp., and Sonic Automotive, Inc., among others. TransDigm, for example, seated nine directors—all male—over the past twelve years.

The state pension funds in Massachusetts, in 2015, and Rhode Island, in 2017, voted against directors up for reelection at companies where women or people of color held less than 25 and 30 percent, respectively, of board directorships. And the California State Teachers' Retirement System (CalSTRS) was considering opposing the reelection of all directors in 2018 at twenty-seven companies without women on their boards.

BlackRock, the world's largest money manager, announced in a set of proxy voting guidelines in February 2018 that it expects its portfolio companies to have diverse boards, with at least two female directors on every board.[247] BlackRock's global head of investment stewardship asked three hundred companies in the Russell 1000 with fewer than two women on the board to disclose their approach to boardroom and employee diversity. BlackRock CEO Larry Fink also insists that these firms explain how they contribute to the betterment of society.

In 2017, asset management firm State Street Corp. began compelling its portfolio companies to improve their boardroom diversity. State Street put its money where its mouth was when it voted against the reelection of directors at some four hundred companies that did not take serious steps to address gender diversity. State Street made a compelling statement about gender diversity on corporate boards when it commissioned "Fearless Girl," a bronze statue that was set to face—or face down—Wall Street's famous "Charging Bull." The fifty-inch-tall statue was designed specifically to call attention to a State Street Global Advisors initiative to increase the number of women on corporate boards. State Street has said that more than 150 companies have added a woman to their boards since "Fearless Girl" took a stand in Manhattan's financial district.[248]

The Business Roundtable, which defines itself as an "association of chief executive officers of leading US companies working to promote a thriving economy and expanded opportunity for all Americans through sound public policy,"[249] published its commitment to boardroom diversity in 2016: "Diverse backgrounds and experiences on corporate boards, including those of directors who represent the broad range of society, strengthen board performance and promote the creation of long-term shareholder value."[250] The Roundtable (a 197-executive-member organization that includes sixteen women)[251] spells out unambiguously what it means by "the broad range of society:" "Boards should develop a framework for identifying appropriately diverse candidates that allows the nominating/corporate governance committee to consider women, minorities and others with diverse backgrounds as candidates for each open board seat."[252] Arguably, no other business group's diversity recommendation carries as much weight as the Roundtable.

In June 2016 General Motors was able to boast an almost even split of men and women on its board.[253] That same year thirteen CEOs signed on to a set of Commonsense Corporate Governance Principles.[254] The second principle, immediately following a call for truly independent corporate boards, is an assertion that diverse boards make better decisions. "Every board should have members with complementary and diverse skills, backgrounds and experiences,"[255] according to the signatories, which include GM's Mary Barra, Berkshire's Warren Buffett, and JPMorgan Chase's Jamie Dimon, among others.

Finally, some organizations—primarily created by women—have sprung up to address gender equity issues.

"At PowHer New York, we have been working at the city and state levels in New York to increase gender diversity on corporate boards,"[256] says PowHer New York founder Beverly Neufeld.

The grassroots network of individuals and organizations that lobbied New York Governor Andrew Cuomo to advance greater representation of women on corporate boards (and in management) is pushing for gender equity not through often unpopular quotas, but through legislative activism.

"In the 'Governor's Report on the Status of New York Women and Girls, 2018 Outlook,' we were able to argue that 'while women make up over half of the US population and nearly half of the corporate workforce, they make up only about 20 percent of corporate boards,"[257] Neufeld says. "Our point is to make change by creating an expectation, not by shouting out a demand."

Even more "PowHer-ful" than her network of one hundred partners, Neufeld believes, is the #MeToo Movement, the worldwide "empowerment through empathy"[258] action to publicize and end workplace sexual violence, most of it directed at women.

"#MeToo may have begun with women's experience of sexual assault in the workplace, but we are now associating it with the need for women's leadership," Neufeld says. "Business is telling women that it needs our help. But how can we help if we don't have a seat at the table? With women on boards, issues of sexual violence and of women's leadership in the workplace and boardroom will be more attended to."[259]

Neufeld believes we are at an unusual moment in time and we need to take advantage of how seriously business is taking the #MeToo voices.

"We may not even need quotas," Neufeld says. "It's just a great time to push."

DirectWomen was founded in 2007 as a project of the American Bar Association and is a nonprofit focused on getting more female attorneys onto corporate boards. The Thirty Percent Coalition is a national organization committed to the goal of women holding 30 percent of board seats. The Executive Leadership Council has a Corporate Board Initiative (CBI) to enhance the preparedness of Black executives for service on corporate boards and the Latino Corporate Directors Association (LCDA) went so far as to create a Latino Board Tracker which measures Latino representation (and the lack thereof) on the boards of the Fortune 1000. And the list goes on.

Women and others who are not well represented in boardrooms are still trying to assess which is the best way to go pragmatically, philosophically, and societally.

* * *

So, which works best? Quotas? Targets? Persuasion?

Women and others who are not well represented in boardrooms are still trying to assess which is the best way to go pragmatically, philosophically, or societally. Did the mandate for more female representation on corporate boards in Norway improve corporate profitability and corporate governance as proponents promised? Some companies saw improvement in both areas—but some didn't. Did the higher female representation on corporate boards improve board decision-making, as supporters claimed? While data suggest that decision-making processes may have changed, the effectiveness of the decisions did not improve just by putting more women on boards.[260] The results in Norway were mixed at best. However, it is acknowledged that at the time their quota was instituted in Norway, the supply of qualified women was limited and the short time frame that was given to make what were quite significant changes to board composition necessitated the occasional suboptimal board appointment.

Certainly the "golden skirts"—the qualified female executives who accumulate directorships in bulk—have found more opportunities and higher pay because of their board appointments. But over-boarding has stretched them thin—a new reality that does not serve women, companies, or shareholders well.

In my view, the jury is still out. The diversity mandates for corporate boards have been around for only fifteen years. Was it humanly possible for companies to reengineer their boards in a decade and a half? Sometimes I think it was. But creating a thoroughly diverse board probably takes more time than that. A new generation of gender and ethnically diverse executives must acquire the strategic thinking and executive experience that are essential for a board directorship. Going forward, corporate mentors and advocates must keep giving these people opportunities to tackle new challenges regarding new markets, profitability, innovation, and many other issues. Women and other diverse executives need to take on increasingly challenging assignments, with P&L responsibility being among the most important.

There is also the all-important question as to who gets included in quotas. Women only? What happens when our pool of executives from whom we obtain board candidates is no longer made up of simply two genders? What about other minority groups so lacking in the boardroom? Is sexual orientation important to board qualifications? And what about age diversity? What and whom should be covered under mandates also depends on where you are in the world. Diversity is defined differently in America versus Argentina versus Australia.

As better qualified women and minorities join corporate boards, data scientists, economists, and management consultants will have to quantify the real-world effects of having women—and minorities—in the boardroom. As management consultant Peter Drucker famously said, "What gets measured gets improved." Amazingly enough, in 2021, it's still early in the push for boardroom diversity. In time, we will be able to measure the impact that women and minorities have on corporate decision-making and ultimately corporate results.

We are ready for the outcomes, whatever they may be.

One thing is certain: The genie is out of the bottle. The pressure to make boardrooms more diverse is out in the open, and it's coming from government, industry, and other grassroots initiatives. It is not going away. Stay tuned.

CHAPTER 11

WE CAN'T FIND QUALIFIED DIVERSE DIRECTORS!

The world as we have created it is a process of our thinking.
It cannot be changed without changing our thinking.

—ALBERT EINSTEIN

When the manager of a baseball team wants to hire a new pitcher, how does he proceed? Does he ask his ballplayers, "Hey, anybody know a good pitcher?"

When the coach of the hockey team needs a defenseman, where does she look?

It hardly bears stating that sports teams are always on the lookout for pitching talent and defensemen, and they designate scouts to travel the country seeking out new prospects. The process is comprehensive and wide-reaching.

When it comes to finding a new board member—a player as important to a company as a pitcher is to his team—the existing board members typically begin by asking each other, "Who do we know?"

When it comes to selecting a woman, or a minority candidate, boards frequently resort to one or two fallback positions: "we can't find them" or "they don't exist."

In September 2020 it was reported that the CEO of Wells Fargo, Charles Scharf, stated that the bank was having trouble reaching its diversity goals because there was not enough qualified minority talent. This was not received well (to say the least). But the truth of the matter is that this thinking is still more common than we would like to believe. Most of the time it simply does not get spoken publicly.

In 2018 the UK Government commissioned a report on gender balance. Focused on the FTSE350, the Hampton-Alexander Review reported some outrageous explanations for the lack of women on these boards:

- "I don't think women fit comfortably into the board environment."

- "There aren't that many women with the right credentials and depth of experience to sit on the board—the issues covered are extremely complex."

- "Most women don't want the hassle or pressure of sitting on a board."

- "All the 'good' women have already been snapped up."[261]

And the list goes on. While this research was based in the UK and focused on gender, there are similar excuses provided with respect to the lack of other types of board diversity.

Is there really a shortage of women and minorities qualified to serve on corporate boards of directors—or do we find endless excuses for maintaining the status quo?

Let me be unequivocal and state that without a shadow of a doubt it is a demand problem and not a supply problem. Again, it is not a supply problem. In fact, I tell my clients to create the dream wish list for their next director, and I will find them several of this type of person to consider AND they will be diverse as well.

So, what is going on?

Turns out that corporate boards may be looking in the wrong places, and they may not be looking hard enough. Finding women, diversity of sexual orientation, or ethnically diverse executives qualified to hold board seats is of course different than zeroing in on a talented pitcher or defenseman. However, they both require diligent proactive effort rather than a passive "who-do-we-know" exercise.

In terms of looking in the wrong places, we know that boards still generally prefer CEOs and former CEOs. But only 7.4 percent of Fortune 500 CEOs are female,[262] and only 29 percent of senior management roles are held by women.[263] The numbers for CEOs who are racially/ethnically diverse are even worse. Currently there are four Black CEOs of Fortune 500 companies[264] and nine Hispanic CEOs.[265] While there are a few Indian American CEOs of Fortune 500 companies, there is currently one from East Asia (China, Japan, Korea).[266] And, at last count, there were three openly gay CEOs of Fortune 500 companies. So when the criterion is limited to CEOs, the pool of qualified and diverse board directors remains small.

Let us look at it a different way: in July 2020 Business Insider published a list of the top twenty-five most innovative chief marketing officers in the world.[267] The CMOs of companies such as AT&T and Amazon are included in this list, so there are ostensibly some potential board possibilities. Of the twenty-five executives on the list, two are female as well as racially/ethnically diverse, another ten are female, and five more are racially/ethnically diverse males. This group of highly accomplished executives is 68 percent diverse. Similar findings will most certainly be discovered when looking at other pools of senior executives outside the corner office.

Who we need for our boardroom and who we know are likely to be different.

We also may not be looking hard enough.

As has been mentioned previously, much of the identification of new board candidates comes from a "who-do-we-know exercise." To be fair, this process may also include requests for recommendations from trusted advisors such as attorneys and bankers, and while this may yield options, it is still insular. Very simply, who we need for our boardroom and who we know are likely to be different. And who we know tends to be people like us. People who look like us, live in the same communities as us, and who have gone to the same schools as us. No wonder our dismay about the lack of diversity.

When a company does decide to be strategic about its board recruiting process, the ritual also tends to insular. The company hires one of four or five large search firms with established board practices. These board practices already know the company in need of the new director. They are also already familiar with "anyone worth knowing." This perpetuates a search process that is exclusive and parochial. In other words, it's a more sophisticated "who-do-we-know exercise" with the addition of outside advisors and a cost of about $100,000 per director search.

Despite the apparent hurdles, the truth is that more than ever before, there are a plethora of qualified candidates who also happen to be diverse. And with all the transparency that technology has delivered, it does not have to be hard to find them. The obstacles lie in the assumptions we make and the excuses we tell ourselves.

There is also the human tendency toward the familiar and the status quo. Einstein purportedly said that insanity is doing the same thing repeatedly and expecting different results. If boards are truly committed to improving diversity among their ranks, then they must not only evolve what is perceived to be the ideal candidate but commit to being open to new ways of identifying and recruiting such candidates. Different fields, different grasshoppers; different seas, different fish (Indonesian proverb).

Part of the tendency to stick with the status quo and the path of least resistance comes not only from what we look for and where and how we look, but also what happens when we find a potentially suitable candidate for our boards.

Our methods of assessment and selection of board directors have not changed much in decades, and they are largely subjective. Sure, there are endless leadership assessment tools, as well as personality and psychometric testing, but when it comes to evaluating potential board directors, there is currently no objective tool that is commonly used. In fact, when I began recruiting board directors twenty-four years ago, an interview was often not even part of the process.

Thankfully, this is no longer the case. We are more thorough than ever before, but being thorough does not equate to being objective. Board candidates typically go through an interview process that is conversational. There are questions and answers, and there may be multiple such interviews. The interview process might begin with the recruiter if there is one involved and proceed to the nominating and governance committee of the board, and eventually the whole board may partake in the process. No matter the number and sequence, in the end, the process is idiosyncratic and not objective.

People prefer hiring people they like, regardless of other qualifications (or the lack thereof). These were the findings of multiple researchers, including Lauren Rivera, associate professor of management and organizations at the Kellogg School of Management at Northwestern University.[268]

Rivera also found that by the time a candidate had made it through the relevant résumé screenings and landed an interview, evaluation was not necessarily based on "maximizing skill—finding the person who was absolutely best at the soft or the hard dimensions of the job," as Rivera puts it. Rather, the most common mechanism by which a candidate was evaluated was her similarity to her interviewer.

It is important to note that much of the interview process is conducted by other board members who, while astute and experienced, have various levels of competency with recruiting and interviewing. They also have various levels of self-awareness and knowledge of their own biases. Thus, in its mere structure, the board interview process is suboptimal, and this can make it more difficult for unfamiliar and diverse directors to succeed in the process.

What if we add some objectivity to the process? Can we employ some of the leading-edge tools and psychometric testing to help create a process that is based on merit and qualifications? We also need to professionalize the interview process. This begins with an awareness that even the most senior and successful executives would benefit from interview guidelines and structure.

Rationalizing a board's homogeneity is becoming harder and harder. In the end, excuses no longer cut it. There are ample qualified board candidates who also happen to be diverse. Changing decades of status quo is not easy but entirely possible. We need to do the heavy lifting that is required to improve corporate boards and move away from the song and dance about there being no candidates.

CHAPTER 12

HOW TO FIX THE PROBLEM

We need to resist the tyranny of low expectations. We
need to open our eyes to the inequality that remains.
We won't unlock the full potential of the workplace
until we see how far from equality we really are.

—SHERYL SANDBERG

Throughout this book we have deliberated on diversity in boardrooms and the lack thereof. We have examined this age-old problem from various angles and through the lens of different groups' experience. From the preceding chapters we can draw several overriding and seemingly basic conclusions:

- Diversity improves business results.

- Despite this, improvements to diversity in boardrooms has been insufficient.

- For a whole host of social, cultural, demographic, and economic reasons, the time to change is now. In other words, time's up. Boards must become more diverse now. The benefits will be far reaching, including a trickle-down effect leading to diversity at other levels within organizations.

It is also time to challenge the misguided and long-held assumptions about board membership:

- a board seat belongs to a director forever.

- qualified female and minority candidates are in short supply.

- once in the boardroom, directors are beyond reproach.

But how can this be achieved? The answer is not simple but certainly well worth the effort. And the status quo is untenable.

I hereby offer a set of solutions that approach the issue from two vantage points: the top down and the bottom up.

Diversity Solutions from the Top Down

1. BE AWARE

Awareness is the first step no matter the vantage point, so let us begin with this. It is astonishing that in 2021 we are still debating the merits of diversity in the boardroom. After years of efforts in this arena, including thousands of articles and conversations, it is still not universally accepted that boards benefit when there are divergent experiences and opinions around the table. In PwC's 2020 Annual Corporate Directors Survey, it was stated that "47% of directors say gender diversity is very important to their boards" and "only 34% of directors believe it is very important to have racial diversity on their board."[269] In this same report 84 percent of directors stated that companies should be doing more to promote diversity in the workplace. Why the discrepancy between workplace and boardroom?

Companies, organizations, and educational institutions everywhere are hiring chief diversity officers. Check the hiring announcements on any random day, and they will be flush with new appointments, job postings, and commitments to improve diversity. This is fabulous news and should be applauded. However, I maintain that to be truly authentic and successful, diversity must begin at the very top of the organization with the board of directors. Senior leadership must also reflect the diversity the company is trying to achieve, but start with the board, and the message becomes crystal clear and implications are indisputable.

Awareness and the change it can catalyze also begins with an appreciation that we all harbor unconscious biases. No matter your gender, age, ethnicity, or personal experience, everyone maintains beliefs about others that are unjust. In fact, the fields of psychology and sociology have long studied this phenomenon, which is referred to as "cognitive bias." "Cognitive biases are often a result of your brain's attempt to simplify information processing. Biases often work as rules of thumb that help you make sense of the world and reach decisions with relative speed."[270] Cognitive biases cause us to draw assumptions about people and situations that are not accurate and perhaps even prejudicial. We may feel comfortable telling ourselves whatever truths feel convenient, but the ultimate result is a distortion of reality.

2. REDEFINE THE ESSENTIALS OF A GREAT BOARD

What makes for a great board? Simple question. But one with a whole host of answers depending on to whom the question is asked. CEOs may want a board that is harmonious and agreeable. Board directors also want collegiality and perhaps those they can learn from and enjoy working with. Investors want prudence and thoughtfulness

There is no one universal definition of a great board, and perhaps there should be.

and, of course, returns. Employees want attention to their concerns and policies and procedures that make for a good work environment and a company with stability and future potential. And so on.

The point is that there is no one universal definition of a great board, and perhaps there should be. Perhaps we need to move beyond the idea that a great board is one that is like-minded and agreeable. Perhaps we need to better appreciate the value of challenging the status quo and constructive debate and deliberation. Perhaps we need to select directors who think more like owners and are unafraid to pursue continuous improvement, no matter how hard it may be.

NYSE Governance Services and RHR International conducted research to determine what board directors themselves thought were the components of a strong board. Their findings, while mostly not surprising, merit mention and are a good reminder. They found that the four keys to success are quality dialogue, diversity among members, effective peer and self-evaluations, and managing CEO succession. While almost no one would argue the validity of these four components of quality boards, companies are vastly different in how they concentrate on these items. Judicious boards must attend to all these elements and commit to a focus on their improvement, in perpetuity.

3. QUALIFICATIONS OF A QUALIFIED DIRECTOR

The path toward improved board diversity must include a recalibration of our ideas of what qualifies someone to be a board director.

There is the lingering belief (still) that board directors must come from the ranks of CEOs and former CEOs. True, every board does need these systems thinkers and generalists. Every board must have those who have managed an organization in its entirety. And most CEOs want other CEOs or those who have previously held the role because they can relate to the challenges and obstacles the CEO faces in ways that those who have not held this position simply cannot.

Acting on a premise that CEOs make the best management and strategic decisions, many board directors have historically welcomed only other CEOs into the boardroom. Researchers at the Stanford Graduate School of Business, however, have written that empirical evidence does not bear out the assumption that CEOs make better directors than do other kinds of executives.

"Studies have found no evidence that a CEO board member positively contributes to future operating performance or decision-making and finds CEO directors are associated with higher CEO pay,"[271] according to Stanford's David F. Larcker and Brian Tayan.

In a 2011 Corporate Board of Directors Survey, Larcker found that 87 percent of surveyed directors believe that "active CEOs are too busy with their own companies to be effective directors." Moreover, 79 percent said that, in practice, active CEOs are no better than non-CEO board members.

The harsh reality is that naming only CEOs to a board of directors will limit the number of women and minorities who can gain a seat. Of the CEOs who lead companies that make up the 2019 Fortune 500 list, only thirty-three are women.[272] There were five Black CEOs of Fortune 500 companies in 2020[273] and nine Hispanics.[274] To increase the number of women and minorities on boards, either more women and minorities need to become CEOs or boards must look to other C-level executives as board candidates.

A CEO with a strong track record of growing a business, improving profitability, or even overseeing transformation is indeed accomplished, and many corporate boardrooms would welcome him or her. But other corporate executives—chief financial officers, for example—are valuable because they too have access to every facet of the corporation and can contribute tremendously to a board of directors. Indeed, many corporate executives have come to view the role of CFO, with its emphasis on a methodical, data-driven approach to decision-making, as basic training for becoming a CEO. Perhaps the best-known instance of a CFO who moved into the role of CEO is Indra Nooyi, PepsiCo's CEO (2006). There have been others. Marcel Smits was promoted from finance chief to CEO at consumer products giant Sara Lee in 2010. ITT's Denise Ramos, who helped develop a plan to spin off the group's water and defense businesses, became CEO in 2011.

Genuinely appreciating the value of expertise beyond CEOs and CFOs will go a long way toward improving the quality of your board and its diversity.

Additionally, we most certainly know that most boards could use additional technology, marketing, and human capital expertise. In fact, according to research conducted by Gartner in September 2020, "driven by the onset of COVID-19, digital technology initiatives will serve as the top strategic business priority for BoDs (boards of directors) over the next two years, followed by customer engagement and managing the remote workforce."[275] Diversity of skill set and experience on boards is critical. Again, depending on the company, the board may need deep expertise in regulatory issues, foreign markets, risk management, technical manufacturing, and more. The point is that there are many ways to configure a boardroom and genuinely appreciating the value of expertise beyond CEOs and CFOs will go a long way toward improving the quality of your board and its diversity.

4. REGULAR REFRESHMENT IS ESSENTIAL

Holding on to a board seat ad infinitum is bad governance.

Plenty of governance experts know this. And they know that only a change in outlook, expectations, and culture will make boardroom seats accessible to currently underrepresented communities. Unfortunately, there is still a prevailing belief that if a director leaves a board before a decade (or two), something is wrong. They did not perform well, there was a personality problem, or maybe a culture mismatch. No matter, the situation is deemed to be suspicious. We do not consider the fact that the rate of change for all businesses is extreme and consequently the expertise the board needs today will change too. We do not consider that such change can clear the way for new ideas. And we do not appreciate that such change can open up opportunity for increased diversity.

There is an underlying expectation that director appointments, while no longer for life, are at the very least long term. Board membership can feel like joining a club, and as is the case with other exclusive clubs, once you get in, you do not want to leave. This thinking is so embedded in board membership that it is unspoken and, in many cases, unconscious. For boards to truly embrace refreshment and all the tools and accoutrements to get there, assumptions and expectations must be adjusted, and an appreciation for the value of change must be developed.

In August of 2016, the *Financial Times* reported that US boards are "maler, staler and frailer" than their European counterparts.[276] In fact, the average director tenure in the US was disclosed to be over eight years, while in the UK this number was just under six years. Tenure is meaningful for several reasons, but importantly director independence naturally diminishes the longer the time spent on a board. In an ISS (Institutional Shareholder Services) 2016–2017 policy survey with investors, 51 percent flagged lengthy average tenure as problematic. Just 11 percent of investors said tenure is not a concern.[277]

In a paper that focused on the link between director tenure and innovation, Ning Jia of the School of Economics and Management at Tsinghua University in Beijing observed that "stagnant boards that are filled with directors with extended tenure fail to refresh themselves in a timely manner, can no longer keep current with technological developments and grow unable to offer new insights into corporate issues ... long executive tenure is often associated with rigidity and a commitment to established policies and practices that potentially kill the entrepreneurial spirit and hinder innovation."[278]

There is increasing awareness of the tendency for directors over time to privilege the concerns of management over the concerns of shareholders. The personal relationships that they build with the CEO (whom they may have hired) and with one another can cause them to lose their independence and objectivity. They may be unable to challenge the CEO during a crisis or speak up when necessary. They may be unable to urge the organization to alter strategic direction.

If directors can be convinced that we all have a shelf life, then board refreshment and turnover could be viewed as beneficial and essential.

To say it another way, knowing when to step down from a board if you are a veteran board member may be the best thing you can do for your company—because stepping down means making room for new people, new ideas, and new directions.

Board refreshment is on the minds of shareholders and regulators. They seek to understand the value and contributions made by the board in its entirety, as well as individual directors. Board refreshment has come to be understood as a best practice of corporate governance. Boards are no longer treated as lifetime appointments, as was the case not too long ago. Yet how to effectuate board refreshment is not straightforward. There is no cure-all, and it is certainly not easy. To make the necessary changes, board refreshment must be an agenda item at board meetings. There are also no hard-and-fast rules, but it can unequivocally be said that it should never be done arbitrarily. The nominating and governance committee is tasked with this responsibility, and it must be afforded the time necessary to do it the right way.

Operationalizing Refreshment: A Step at a Time

Board refreshment should not be some random formulaic activity. It must be judicious, thoughtful, and relevant to the company's overall objectives and strategy. Changing directors simply to change them makes no sense.

The exercise of creating a board matrix that lists directors on one axis and their skills and competencies on the other can allow a board to begin to understand themselves and enumerate their areas of proficiency or lack thereof. The list of skills and competencies should contain those necessary for the future of the business and not only those that are currently present on the board. For example, perhaps the company is moving into a new emerging market, such as Africa. Experience running a business in this region may be a new skill to include on the board matrix. Social media or cybersecurity expertise are recognized and in-demand skills and might be something to consider including on any matrix. For most companies, if these skills are not currently present on the board, they will need to add them sometime soon.

Ultimately, there will be many opinions about how and when refreshment should take place and who is to be refreshed. For example, Warren Buffett has been on the Berkshire Hathaway board for fifty-six years, and Rupert Murdoch was on Twenty-First Century Fox (previously 20th Century Fox) for thirty-one years. Should they step down from these roles to make room for new talent?

Fresh perspectives can be very valuable when trying to solve any problem or make important decisions. On the other hand, long tenured experience and expertise contribute clarity and, of course, wisdom. The right combination of these attributes can be difficult to obtain, but difficulty should not discourage trying. Boards have not always been proactive about their own evolution and effectiveness. However, they no longer have much of a choice. Boards need to become more self-aware. Complacency and being opaque about their internal workings are things of the past.

The word *refreshment* of course conjures up the word *fresh,* and one look at the definition of *fresh* should make any doubt surrounding refreshment dissipate: Fresh: having its original qualities unimpaired such as (1) full of or renewed in vigor, (2) not stale, sour, or decayed (3) not faded (Merriam-Webster dictionary).

Can your company afford anything less?

5. BOARD EVALUATIONS ARE NOT OPTIONAL

The foremost criteria when reviewing any board and board member must be contribution and performance. Prior accomplishments, fame, and notoriety are nice, but shareholders and stakeholders deserve much more than mere prominence. They merit true effort and engagement. As such, before any board refreshment exercise, a full and thorough board evaluation should be conducted. The New York Stock Exchange requires boards of publicly traded companies to evaluate their own performance at least once a year to see whether they are functioning effectively. Yet a 2017 study published by *Harvard Business Review* found that evaluations of 187 surveyed boards were largely "inadequate." Additionally, some 55 percent of companies that do conduct board evaluations rated individual directors, and only 36 percent said their company did a "very good job" of accurately assessing individual director performance.

There are all sorts of methodologies that can be used, but the goal should be a comprehensive and objective enumeration of individual director performance. Interestingly, from almost the moment one enters school and then the work force, performance evaluations (they start as report cards in school) are commonplace and expected. Yet at the board level, until recently, directors were usually considered beyond evaluation. Among the S&P 1500 firms, board evaluations are now close to universal (97 percent, according to a survey conducted by ISS—Institutional Shareholder Services). However, according to the PWC 2016 Annual Corporate Directors Survey, only 49 percent said their board actually made changes because of their self-evaluation. Board evaluations cannot be a box-checking exercise. Rather, their value and purpose must be understood, and the results should bring about meaningful change and improvement.

At present, there is no consistent board evaluation process. Some companies do self-evaluations of the board in its entirety, and some have directors evaluate their own performance. Often, evaluations include a basic checklist review of board structures and processes or questionnaires filled out by individual directors. The data is typically synthesized by the company's general counsel or outside legal counsel and reported back to the board. Evaluations of individual directors, their contributions to corporate strategy, and their interactions with other board members are usually "not performed in a rigorous manner." This is because many board members do not see the value of stringent evaluations, so they do not expend the time or effort needed to fully engage in the process. Nor do they promote the notion. There is also legacy thinking that becoming a director is enough proof of competence and performance. This goes back to the days when most board directors were CEOs or former CEOs. Today, we have more varied experiences on the board, and as such, the necessity for some form of performance assessment has never been greater.

Also, it should be noted that the very definition of what constitutes excellent board performance remains ambiguous. I have worked with many companies and board directors trying to determine what actually constitutes board performance beyond attendance and speaking up. Views on this remain inconsistent.

Board evaluations cannot be conducted in a vacuum. They must take into consideration the unique circumstances of the board and company in question. This should include consideration of the company's strategy. What are the near- and medium-term goals and challenges, and does the board have the requisite skills to guide the company appropriately? The competitive environment needs to be considered, as do expectations from investors. To evaluate the board is to consider risks the company faces and make a determination that the board is equipped not only to plan for them but also to properly react if the worst-case scenario comes to pass. Many discussions of board refreshment do not include board evaluation, as if they are separate aspects of the functioning of the board. To effectively refresh one must effectively evaluate first.

Board evaluations can help pave the way for board refreshment. Age limits and term limits are additional means of refreshing a board. There are many diverging opinions as to the effectiveness of these "forced exit" mechanisms. It is often argued that experienced directors add value and that there is little to compare to the wisdom and institutional knowledge that comes with time spent affiliated with a board. Nevertheless, according to the 2016 Deloitte Board Practices Report, among large cap companies, 81 percent have age limits and 5 percent have term limits. In midcap companies, 74 percent have age limits, and 6 percent have term limits.

Despite the prevalence of age limits, directorships in the S&P 1500 held by seventy-something board members rose from 11.7 percent in 2008 to 18.6 percent in 2016. Those eighty and above represented 1.8 percent in 2016. Again, it is performance that matters. There is an expression "It's not the age, it's the sage."

It should be noted that, as previously mentioned in this book, a board that is entirely composed of a particular generation may suffer from the same lack of diversity limitations that boards without gender or ethnic diversity do.

As for term limits, all the large cap companies that do have them specify a maximum term of between twelve and fifteen years. Notably, and not surprisingly, according to a study by the Investor Responsibility Research Center Institute (IRRC) and ISS, "term limits led to a meaningful decrease in average board tenure and younger directors, and it is the most effective tool if the goal is to ensure board turnover."[279]

It should also be noted that there are some practical considerations that need to be included in any discussion about board refreshment. Board committee structure and participation will impact the amount of refreshment that a board undertakes. It has been shown that "service on the nominating, audit, and compensations committees may lead to longer tenures due to the desire to retain subject-matter expertise."[280]

6. BOARD SUCCESSION PLANNING

Effective board refreshment goes hand in hand with board succession planning. Like board refreshment, succession planning is also a relatively new proceeding for corporate boards. The Council of Institutional Investors (CII), which is a nonprofit with members who have combined assets that exceed $3 trillion, "maintains that boards should implement and disclose a board succession plan that involves preparing for future board retirements, committee assignment rotations, committee chair nominations, and overall implementation of the company's long-term business plan."

Board succession planning, like all other business succession planning, is part of sound organizational foresight and risk management. A robust and regular board succession planning process focuses the board on its future. Through deliberate thinking about where the company is heading strategically, as well as the challenges it will encounter along the way, boards can prepare to recruit the requisite skills and experiences necessary to guide the company into its future. A board that is planning for succession is inherently planning for refreshment. In other words, refreshment is a natural by-product of board succession planning.

Like CEO succession planning, board succession planning allows the company to move from reactive to proactive. It permits the company to identify new board directors in advance of when they are needed and takes away the urgency of making a decision, any decision, due to a ticking clock. Years ago, before it was even defined as such, I remember a client of mine asking me to identify directors with a particular skill set and current on-the-ground experience in Asian emerging markets. This was a year or so before they anticipated bringing such a person onto the board. Given the geographical divide and very particular set of skills they were looking for, this was a sound strategy. The goal was to identify qualified directors in countries such as Thailand and Vietnam and begin discussions about potentially, eventually joining their board. Not only did this board succession planning allow us to dig deeply into these faraway regions of the world, but there was ample time for referencing and other checks and balances that are required when recruiting directors who are completely unfamiliar.

So, what should an effective board succession plan entail? To plan for the board's future, we must begin in the present. The board must have a clear and unbiased understanding of its current composition. This means: What are its strengths, and where are its weaknesses or gaps? The point is the board must be able to make an objective assessment of itself, its skills, expertise, and competencies. The tool that is most often used is the board matrix, illustrated on the next page and originally referred to on page 81.

This snapshot of the board will help visualize the areas where the board may be lacking expertise. This is particularly powerful when gauged against the company strategy. The company can then look at when directors will be retiring and plan for its future. Let us look at an example of how this plays out. Here is a sample board matrix similar to the ones I create for my clients. For illustration purposes we will say this is a consumer-packaged-goods company with a global footprint.

THE CONSUMER COMPANY BOARD MATRIX

Name/Title	Age	Tenure	Diversity	Active/Retired	Operating Exp.	Financial Expert	Industry Experience	Manufacturing	Global Exp.	Technology
Christina Audley	63	10	F	R	✓	✓	✓			
Gertrude Cole	57	7	F	A		✓		✓		✓
Tyler Gordon	55	8		A	✓	✓	✓	✓		
Cate Harris	60	12	F/E	A	✓	✓	✓		✓	
Gregory Perdue	71	18		R	✓	✓				
Jason Smith	66	10		R	✓	✓		✓		
Quinn Waters	49	6		A		✓	✓			

As can be seen in the above matrix, this company is lacking in global experience and technology, broadly defined.

The next step is to look at anticipated retirements. According to PWC, 71 percent of S&P 500 companies report having a mandatory retirement age for directors. For those boards, 46 percent set their retirement age at seventy-five or higher.[281] The board must look at likely and upcoming retirements and what expertise the board will lose with each director who leaves the board. We then can create an annual schedule (a five-year plan probably suffices for the purposes of this exercise) of future gaps on the board. As we do this, we must keep in mind evolution of the company and its strategy. Some skills that vacate the board may no longer need replacement. This might look something like this:

Year	Board retirements	Skills and experiences going off the board
2022	Gregory Perdue	-operating -financial
2023	Cate Harris	-operating -financial -Industry -global
2024 and beyond...		

Through this exercise we can plan for succession in a strategic manner. We can be proactive and really take a deep dive into how the board's composition will evolve. In terms of the example above, we see that the very limited global experience on this board will depart in 2023 and it would be important to plan for and not only replace this experience but possibly add additional global experience as well.

This practice can be applied to board committees, as well, so that we create a road map for properly configuring these work groups of the board. Many times, committee composition is almost an afterthought, and the implementation of thorough and regular board succession planning helps do away with this suboptimal practice. We move from the tactical to the strategic.

To be clear, I am not saying that boards need to be in a state of constant renewal. Optimally speaking, a third of the board should be new. a third should be medium term, and a third should be long term—directors in their tenth, eleventh, or twelfth year of board service. If you have turnover, you have more open seats, and more opportunity to bring in new women, minorities, and yes, White men, with expertise in technology, social media, and global trade. This must, of course, always be counterbalanced with institutional knowledge and wisdom that comes from directors who have been around for a while.

Here are some of the leading best practices for board succession planning:

- Begin with a matrix that plots directors on one axis and skills and qualifications on the others. The types of skills and qualifications should evolve as the company does, and doing this objectively will make clear gaps in expertise on the board.

- Board succession planning must be regular and taken seriously. It may be difficult to initiate but well worth the effort in the long run.

- Board succession planning should include succession planning for board committees. Boards must also prepare for changes in committee chairs.

- Once the analysis of the current board is done and gaps are understood, make sure the process for identifying and appointing new board members is strategic, objective, and based on the needs of the organization. Do not cut corners because someone knows someone or there is impatience with the process.

- Prepare for onboarding new board members in a manner similar to that of onboarding an employee. Directors need to understand the organization's structure, culture, strengths, weaknesses, and opportunities. They must be provided with the tools and information to succeed.

- Mentor new board members to prepare them for leadership within the board, so a framework for the transfer of power is in place before it is needed.

- Conduct robust annual performance evaluations of boardrooms and individual board directors, facilitated, if necessary, by an independent third party.

- Expect the unexpected. Develop an emergency succession plan in the event that a board chairman or director needs to vacate his or her seat without advance notice.

The board chair and the head of the nominating and governance committee should technically lead a director search process. CEOs should limit their involvement, but in reality, they are usually very engaged. Be aware of who wields the power and make sure decision-making is equitable.

7. ABOVE ALL, CULTURE

"Culture eats strategy for breakfast."

These famous words from Peter Drucker are as relevant today as always. They are particularly meaningful within the context of our conversation about how to achieve diversity in organizations and ultimately in boardrooms. "If you have a great culture, your people will develop a strategy that will win. But if you don't have a good culture, even a winning strategy will not be useful."[282] This holds true for overall company strategy as well as diversity strategy.

Organizational culture is largely invisible, but it is embedded everywhere. The first step toward creating a culture that values and embeds diversity is to understand what exists currently. Understanding the current culture for better or for worse needs to be done before change can occur. Once current culture is assessed, future culture must be defined. For an organization to attempt to improve its diversity without first creating the environment for success is like building a house without a foundation.

So, what does the culture feel like in an organization that values diversity? The Society for Human Resources Management describes several components of such workplaces:

Celebrate Employee Differences: One of the most important ways to show employees that you respect their backgrounds and traditions is to invite them to share those in the workplace.

Listen to Employees: Conduct a comprehensive assessment of your organization's demographics and people processes to develop specific strategies to promote inclusiveness.

Communicate Goals and Measure Progress: Establish and clearly communicate specific, measurable, and time-bound goals as you would with any other strategic aim.[283]

A culture of diversity begins with self-awareness and objectivity. It takes into account embedded bias and the tendency to rely on age-old ways of doing things. It then progresses in ways that may at times feel uncomfortable but always considers best practices and the ultimate benefit that ensues from change.

Diversity Solutions from the Bottom Up

8. IT ALL BEGINS WITH EDUCATION

There is no way to fully do justice to the idea that education impacts everything.

However, in the context of this book, we must recognize that any discussion of diversity in boardrooms must remember that the pipeline requires constant replenishment, and this starts decades before any notion of careers and boards are even an abstraction.

According to the National Education Association, "research shows that providing a high-quality education for children before they turn five yields significant medium—and long-term benefits for students."[284] In 2018 the Organisation for Economic Cooperation and Development (the OECD) published a paper called "The Power and Promise of Early Learning." Researchers Elizabeth A. Shuey and Miloš Kankaraš found that "the first five years of children's lives are critical to their development. During this period, children learn at a faster rate than at any other time in their lives, developing cognitive and social and emotional skills that are fundamental to their future achievements throughout childhood and as adults. These skills are also the foundation for general well-being—laying the groundwork for how individuals cope with successes and setbacks, both professionally and in their personal lives."[285]

While there is continuing debate in the US about the quality of our education system, continued progress in graduation rates from high school and colleges are a key step in sustaining a diverse professional workforce. According to the National Center for Education Statistics, high school graduation rates in the United States have improved from 78 percent in 2009–2010 to 85 percent in 2017–2018.[286]

Although African American and Hispanic graduation rates are below those of Asians and Whites, progress is evidenced across all categories of the broad ethnicity spectrum. Perhaps not surprisingly since they lagged significantly below Asian and White graduation rates, the most improvement in graduation rates for a longer period, since 2000, was for Hispanics and African Americans, with increases in graduation rates of 25 percent and 8 percent respectively.[287]

Similarly, college graduation rates show the same trend. According to the Status and Trend Report (2018) from the National Education Center for Education Statistics, from the period of 2000–2001 to 2015–2016, the number of bachelor's degrees granted to Hispanic people more than tripled and increased by 75 percent for Black people while only increasing by 29 percent for White people.[288]

These improvements are heartening, and the momentum must continue. The more we can begin at the beginning, the more options we create. This is true for both for individual potential as well as the organizations looking to diversify their ranks.

9. RECRUITMENT, INCLUSION, AND RETENTION

While it is not surprising to see progress in educational attainment, as we have explained throughout this book, we require a more sustained effort by organizations to recruit, include, and retain a diverse workforce. These are the building blocks for ensuring diversity in the boardroom.

Robust human capital efforts in organizations need to begin at the outset. This means recruitment that is inclusive at the most junior levels of the organization. This requires forethought and planning. It requires screening processes that are mindful of the potential for bias and interviewers who are diverse themselves. Internships and college-alumni recruitment efforts are often cited as simple and cost-effective methods to diversify talent pools. Dedication and engagement from the top of the company is critical for these efforts to be successful: senior executives must "walk the talk" and demonstrate by example, year in and year out, that such programs matter, that diversity is a core value of the organization.

A diverse workforce must be the goal of recruitment at all levels of the organization. This includes initiatives at the mid and senior executive levels. This can result in a virtuous circle of improving diversity. When entry level employees see diversity in the executive ranks, they know there is room for them to grow within the organization. This will lead to more entry level diversity, leading to more overall diversity, leading to executive level diversity, and so on.

Diversity is a seat at the table, and inclusion is speaking up and being heard.

Diversity and inclusion are often lumped together in conversations and corporate initiatives; however, they do not automatically occur together. The common refrain is that diversity is a seat at the table, and inclusion is speaking up and being heard. Diversity is more measurable; inclusion is not. The Centre for Global Inclusion provides excellent definitions:

> **Diversity** refers to the variety of similarities and differences among people, including but not limited to gender, gender identity, ethnicity, race, native or indigenous origin, age, generation, sexual orientation, culture, religion, belief system, marital status, parental status, socio-economic difference, appearance, language and accent, disability, mental health, education, geography, nationality, work style, work experience, job role and function, thinking style, and personality type.

Inclusion is a dynamic state of operating in which diversity is leveraged to create a fair, healthy, and high-performing organization or community. An inclusive environment ensures equitable access to resources and opportunities for all. It also enables individuals and groups to feel safe, respected, engaged, motivated, and valued, for who they are and for their contributions toward organizational and societal goals.[289]

A full examination of this complex topic is beyond the scope of this book. However, it is important to realize that while diversity is an important goal, it only goes part of the way toward solving what we are trying to solve. To fully benefit from the diversity we have been discussing throughout this book, people must feel accepted and included for who they are. They must be able to bring their full and authentic selves to the workplace. "Identity cover" is a term used in the diversity and inclusion community to refer to employees hiding parts of themselves at work out of fear and discomfort. Examples include "a Muslim who prays in his car because he doesn't want to advertise his religion, a mother who doesn't put up pictures of her children so that coworkers won't question her commitment to the job, or a gay executive who is unsure whether he can bring his partner to company functions."[290] In these examples, the organization may get the credit for diversity, but they do not get the benefits. To achieve the latter, employee contributions to the conversation must be based on their genuine opinions and thought processes and not necessarily those of the larger majority. In this way we cultivate environments that not only value diversity from the outside, but more importantly, from the inside.

It is one thing to recruit a work force that is diverse and to pay attention to issues of inclusion, but it is quite another to retain these individuals and move them up within the organization.

In 2017 The Kapor Center and Harris Poll surveyed a representative sample of more than two thousand US adults who have left a job in a technology-related industry or function within the last three years. Key findings included the fact that "nearly 40 percent of employees surveyed indicated that unfairness or mistreatment played a major role in their decision to leave their company, and underrepresented men were most likely to leave due to unfairness."[291]

Diversity and inclusion initiatives go only part of the way if the organization is unable to retain their diverse employees. Put another way, if we pay attention to return on investment of these initiatives, we realize that to be financially meaningful and have a positive impact on organizations, the people that we recruit and include must also be retained. Furthermore, if we are truly improving diversity in the boardroom, we must create environments in which the best talent rises through the organization. The environment must encourage opportunities for improvement and for growth for all of the most talented.

We end this important chapter with a simple model on the next page that demonstrates the perpetual nature of improving diversity in boardrooms. To illustrate, a diverse executive pool leads to diverse boards which leads to a culture of diversity which will lead to entry level diversity which brings about more diverse executives.

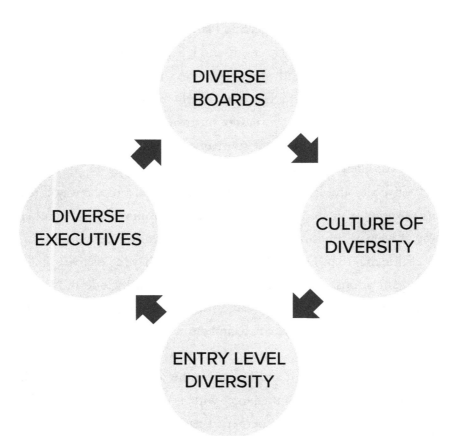

No matter which step in this virtuous cycle one begins with, each moves the organization in the right direction, toward diversity in the boardroom and ultimately at all levels of the organization.

CHAPTER 13

SOME FINAL THOUGHTS

To improve is to change; to be perfect is to change often.

—WINSTON CHURCHILL

moved to New York from my hometown of Montreal in 1997 and immediately began working in the executive search business. My boss and mentor at Heidrick & Struggles hired me as her associate, and from day one I worked alongside her to search for superlative CEOs and board directors. In the twenty-four years since I met her, I have conducted over 350 board searches. Candidates I vetted objectively as well as intuitively have taken up positions in corporate boardrooms and the C-suites at Fortune 500 companies, start-ups, and rehabilitated organizations fresh out of bankruptcy court. I made matches in various corners of the world, including Canada, the US, Europe, and Israel. To this day, finding the right people feels like solving a puzzle with dozens of moving parts: someone critically important is missing, and it is my job to find him or her.

How lucky I have been! One day I am having lunch with a woman who is investing in artificial intelligence in the entertainment industry. Another day I am sitting down with a CEO whose ambition is to scale

Mount Kilimanjaro. The people I encounter through search do not suffer fools kindly, and when I present myself as the person who can help them find their next CEO or board director, I had better be on my A game. It's because of them that I set out to write a book insisting that the board director search process be better than it is today and, with that, it would lead to the leadership gems hidden in plain sight: women, Black people, Hispanics, Asians, LGBTQ+ people, and Native Americans (this list is not meant to be exhaustive) whose innovative and administrative genius is too often untapped and unrewarded.

It is amazing to me that more people are not talking about the need for intelligent boardroom search, because the problem is staring us right in the eye. Ever wonder why the Elliott Managements and Starboard Values of the world get into pitched battles with global corporate giants? It's at least in part because of weak governance. Too many boards are not balancing the interests of a company's stakeholders: shareholders, customers, employees, and investors, to name a few. Some board directors have become dead weight by dint of being on a board too long. Some may have operated effectively in the analog era but are simply bewildered by an interconnected digital world whose technologies and business models seem to change by the minute. Thank you, activist investors, for helping get the word out that boards must evolve. The world we live in is fissionable, combustible, and ever-changing. A homogeneous board that still believes that life today is pretty much as it was in the 1990s is unrealistic and doomed to fail.

The burden of proof has been met, diverse boards make better decisions and lead to improved company performance.

This is why, after twelve-plus years of working at the largest executive search firms in the world, I ventured out on my own. As with my previous search work, I am committed to helping companies build strong boardrooms and strong executive suites. And one of the best ways I can deliver on my promise to match companies with the best executives and directors is to introduce talented, data-driven, creative, and accomplished businesspeople and make sure diversity is embedded in every search that I conduct.

The burden of proof has been met, diverse boards make better decisions and lead to improved company performance.

Yet despite research, validation, and prodding by institutional investors, activist shareholders, and advocacy organizations, a startling 13.4 percent of Russell 3000 companies do not yet have a single woman on their board. And the total share of women board directors in Russell 3000 companies is a mere 18.5 percent, an increase of 4.2 percent since 2016. The percentage of African Americans, Hispanics, and Asians is abysmally low too. "Only about 10 percent of S&P500 companies explicitly disclose individual directors' race (ethnicity) and 8 out of 10 of those board members are white."[292]

What is holding corporate America back from the progress we desperately need in the boardroom, the C-suite, the workplace, and a complex, diverse world? Let me offer up and reiterate explanations, gleaned from hundreds of interactions with some of the most creative, hard-driving people at the world's top companies.

There remains a belief is that there are simply not enough qualified diverse candidates to fill board seats. When Twitter went public in 2013 without one woman on its board, the CEO defended himself by saying he could not find women who had the technical skills necessary to understand what their company was about. Turns out that most of the men on the Twitter board didn't have those technical skills either. When a hue and cry went out in response to the all-male board, the CEO was forced to pay attention. In the seven plus years since Twitter's IPO, four staggeringly talented women have been seated in the boardroom. Kudos to Twitter for addressing the company's challenges—and doing the right thing for its shareholders, employees, and tweeters.

Women and minorities are out there, climbing the corporate ladder, founding start-ups, developing complex financial models and products that save lives. They are serving as company spokespeople, drumming up sales, and creating results. It is incumbent on those of us working on board searches and with boards to embrace the value of diverse thinking, whether it comes from a director who is an ethnic/racial minority or from a different generation or geography.

We must also expose the problems behind the mistaken belief that board-ready women and minorities are in short supply. Take a look at the women and minorities who "suddenly" popped up in corporate boardrooms: Debra L. Lee, former chairman and CEO of BET, the parent company of Black Entertainment Television; Dame Marjorie Morris Scardino, former CEO of Pearson and former board chair of the MacArthur Foundation and the Carter Center; Safra A. Catz, co-CEO of Oracle and board director at the Walt Disney Company; Jose Luis Prado, board director of Hormel Foods and Northern Trust. Does this very short list indicate an undersupply of qualified and diverse board candidates?

At the same time, we need to make conscious efforts to fill the pipeline. Corporate executives should be identifying talented employees in the early stages of their careers. As for diverse employees, they need to work toward positions at the highest levels, gaining operational experience as much as possible. If no one is advocating for them, they must advocate for themselves so that they can gain experience with decision-making activities that will benefit them in the boardroom.

Maybe the process by which board directors are recruited is the most important factor. Research shows that 70 percent of directorships are filled through word of mouth or personal networks. This means that the board, CEO, and trusted advisors ask each other who can make a good addition to the board. The main qualification might be that somebody in the inner circle knows this new person and can vouch for him (and, as investor Aileen Lee says, it is usually a "him"). This process is not objective, and it sure isn't strategic. The result will be safe but not optimal.

To get the most qualified directors for your boardroom, you need to see past the "usual suspects"—the people who look, sound, and think like you.

In 30 percent of board searches, the company will engage the services of an executive search firm. Doing so is an improvement over the hit-or-miss of personal networking, but it's not foolproof either. All search firms are not created equal, especially when it comes to diversity. I say this humbly: identifying, evaluating, and recruiting a director is hard work. Done right, it is quite labor intensive, particularly when making the effort to identify and assess candidates who have not been directors previously. The wealth of companies and industries hinges on making the right matches.

If you garner one takeaway from *Time's Up*, it's this: be strategic and proactive about board recruiting. Asking your fellow board directors who they think would make a nice addition to the boardroom is no way to plan for your company's strategic direction for the next ten years or, frankly, the next six months. Sports teams don't build themselves randomly and blithely, and neither should you. Every boardroom search demands a diligent and robust search process. To get the most qualified directors for your boardroom, you need to see past the "usual suspects"—the people who look, sound, and think like you. Every boardroom search needs to include an investigation into qualified, diverse candidates. That's what Dan Rooney, former owner of the Pittsburgh Steelers, decided when he announced in 2003 that NFL teams with head-coach and general-manager vacancies would interview at least one minority candidate.[293] The rule had a profound impact on the NFL: by the start of the 2006 season, the overall percentage of Black coaches had jumped to 22 percent, up from 6 percent before the rule went into effect.[294] And it has now made its way into the business world where the Rooney Rule is an oft referred to convention when trying to implement diversity initiatives.

A second takeaway: the board seat is not yours in perpetuity. Once you settle in, begin to think about your tenure—and what are the experiences and expertise necessary for the candidate who will take your place when the time is right. Perhaps corporate boards can take a page from the US Constitution. The twenty-second amendment ratified in 1951 states that no person shall be elected to the office of the President more than twice.

The key to successful succession planning in the boardroom is firstly that it takes place. Beyond this it must be consistent and dynamic.

* * *

Let's now take a brief look at how aspiring directors can prepare and position themselves so that when boards practice what is preached in this book, these individuals will be ready.

Would-be directors often have many questions about how to attain the elusive and seemingly unattainable corporate board role. After years of individual conversations providing such advice and numerous public presentations on the topic, I herein offer seven suggestions. These come as a result of my twenty-four years of recruiting board directors and from infinite conversations with those who already sit on boards and other experts in the field. By no means are these seven recommendations comprehensive. They are elemental and an essential starting point.

1. Manage your career. Sarbanes-Oxley. Dodd-Frank. Activist investors. All of these have made boards far more scrutinized and regulated than ever. As a result, new board members need very specific skills and qualifications. What has not changed, however, is the fact that operating skills are still sought after in corporate board members.

Other expertise is also definitely required on boards—and in demand. Think financial expertise, risk management, international experience, and technology skills.

Whatever your area of concentration, work exceptionally hard and be successful. Keep your head down in your job, and make progress with positions of increasing responsibility. Become a known expert in your field and advance. You will not get a seat in the boardroom without a track record of success.

2. Build financial skills and knowledge. For those of you who are not CFOs, treasurers, and auditors, you need to acquire some basic financial fluency. Know how to read and understand financial statements. Learn what kinds of questions to ask and when to ask them. All directors must be able to think critically and analytically about financials.

3. Be well-versed about corporate governance. Know how to answer these questions:

- What are the main responsibilities of the board of directors?

- What are the characteristics of a good director?

- What are the common board committees and what are their functions?

- What constitutes a good board?

- What are the most pressing issues boards are facing?

Nothing screams "stop" faster than a potential board candidate who cannot say why he or she wants to be a board member or what a well-functioning board looks like. Joining a board of directors is much more than an entrée into a private club!

4. Develop a clear articulation of your brand/value proposition. Do some soul searching and some research so that you will be able to answer these questions:

- What is your unique personal brand and value proposition for a prospective board?

- What are your key and specific areas of expertise?

- What kind of board do you want to be on? Consider industry, size, stage of company, geography, public vs. private. There are plusses and minuses for both.

- How much capacity do you have?

- How far and how often are you willing and able to travel?

5. Build a strong network. After having done all the above, landing a board seat can be a matter of having the right contacts. Although it has been clear throughout this book that I am a strong proponent of strategic and professionally run board searches, the reality is that board opportunities can still come from almost anywhere. So, let your relevant and existing network know you are interested in a board seat. Pay particular attention to lawyers, accountants, and bankers. These trusted advisors are still often asked for board recommendations by their corporate clients.

It goes without saying that you must return calls from executive recruiters. Even if you are not interested in the search they are currently working on, develop a dialogue and a relationship with recruiters. They just might have a board opportunity for you in the near future.

Private equity firms, venture capitalists, and other institutional investors may also be a source of board opportunities. Their investments and portfolio companies have boards, and they often tap into their own network when an opening comes up.

6. Start small. A nonprofit board may be a good entrée into board service and allow you to hone your director skills. The right nonprofit board can teach valuable governance lessons. Ideally, you will want to join the board of an organization whose mission you believe in. In addition, look for a board that is professional and populated with executives and other professionals you can learn from and with whom you can establish ongoing relationships.

Small companies and start-ups offer another opportunity to begin your board director career. Board work for small companies will be less systematic and straightforward than large, very prescribed public-company board service, and it is exactly this type of challenge that will acclimate you to the boardroom world. Even an advisory board can serve as a training ground and offer you credibility.

Don't just sit back and watch. Let your fellow board members see how competent and knowledgeable you are.

7. Start young. All the preceding actions take time. Begin thinking about board membership early in your career. The great news is that, with the need for technology and social-media expertise, boards may want to appoint younger directors. In short, there's no time like the present.

* * *

If you are a current board director looking to add another board to your portfolio, make sure you are ready by asking yourself these questions:

- **Are you prepared for the intellectual challenge of an additional board directorship?** Boards focus on strategic planning, CEO succession planning, M&A, IT investments, and much more. Each one of these is complex and multifaceted and subject to major implications. Tackling them requires immersion and effort.

- **Can you handle the publicity that comes with an enhanced business profile?** Sitting on an additional board may result in publicity, potentially positive but also negative if something goes wrong—or even if it doesn't. In today's 24/7 news cycle, everything is transparent, and your reputation can be affected.

- **Are you willing to view board service as an opportunity to "give back?"** One basic by-product of board membership is income. However, in the case of start-ups or smaller company boards, compensation may be minimal, even nonexistent. Your chief motivation will be in the expertise and experience you contribute for the sake of growing a fledgling business. (in the case of nonprofits, your motivation must be something other than money.)

When I began recruiting board directors, compensation was not the primary incentive for board candidates. Most directors were CEOs or retired CEOs who emphasized that compensation was not a factor in their joining a board. Of course, compensation for directors twenty years ago was considerably less than it is today. Towers Watson, a risk management and human resource consulting firm, reports that median director compensation in the Fortune 500 was $267,500 in 2017, up 3 percent from the previous year.[295] From May 2018 through May 2019, total average compensation for S&P 500 nonemployee directors was $304,856.[670] Of course, most companies are not in the Fortune 500, and board compensation is not as lucrative. Yet being a board director certainly can supplement your income.

- **What is your motivation for adding a new board?** If your key motivator is ego, think twice about assuming a board seat. Being a good board director takes a lot of work and responsibility. Boardroom service is not a personal feel-good opportunity but rather a job with roles and responsibilities that deal with serious legal, fiduciary, and ethical issues. Thousands, even millions of people are depending on you.

* * *

How Can You Help?

In short, you can help fix the problem of nondiverse boards by becoming an open-minded, intellectually curious individual who delights in working with talented people across a wide range of expertise.

You can help fix the problem of nondiverse boards by understanding that heterodox thinking can help make your company more innovative, more profitable, and more representative of its shareholders, employees, and customers.

You can help fix the problem of nondiverse boards by acknowledging that boards are, at their core, groups of people and as such can benefit from decades of research into group psychology and group dynamics. Keep in mind that people tend to feel threatened by those who do not agree with them. Remember that you are part of a team and that each member brings distinct knowledge and skills; you are not in competition with one another but are working toward a common goal.

You can help fix the problem of nondiverse boards by understanding that everything, including board tenure, has a shelf life.

You will be better for your self-knowledge and openheartedness, as will your fellow board members—and the company you seek to serve.

Time's up for board directors who sit on corporate boards long after they should.

Time's up for boards that do not take an objective approach to the decisions they make for the future of the company and its shareholders.

Time's up for board searches that cut corners.

Time's up for board searches that include only the obvious candidates.

Time's up for excuses.

The time to embrace an agile way of thinking about board membership is now.

Time's Up has clearly and unequivocally demonstrated the business case for diversity at every level of the organization. Companies cannot afford to wait any longer to bring women, minorities, and diversity of sexual orientation into the boardroom.

What are you waiting for?

ENDNOTES

1   Roger C. Mayer, Richard S. Warr, and Jing Zhao, "Do Pro-Diversity Policies Improve Corporate Innovation?" *Financial Management*, January 29, 2018, http://onlinelibrary.wiley.com/doi/10.1111/fima.12205/full.

2   C. Jose Garcia Martin and Begona Herrero, "Boards of Directors: composition and the effects of the performance of the firm," *Economic Research-Ekonomska Istraživanja*, 31, no. 1 (May 1, 2018), https://www.tandfonline.com/doi/full/10.1080/1331677X.2018.1436454.

3   Mallory Schlossberg, "Why Urban Outfitters' Boys' Club Is a Problem," Racked, May 4, 2017, https://www.racked.com/2017/5/4/15547094/urban-outfitters-board-male-white-old.

4   Mark Misercola, "Higher Returns with Women in Decision-Making Positions," Credit Suisse, https://www.credit-suisse.com/corporate/en/articles/news-and-expertise/higher-returns-with-women-in-decision-making-positions-201610.html.

5   Egon Zehnder, "2016 Global Board Diversity Analysis," https://www.egonzehnder.com/GBDA.

6   Lydia DePillis, "When Executives Misbehave, All-Male Boards Are Part of the Problem," CNN Money, October 10, 2017, http://money.cnn.com/2017/10/10/news/companies/harvey-weinstein-sexual-harassment-corporate-boards/index.html.

7   California Resolution 62, July 11, 2013, http://www.leginfo.ca.gov/pub/13-14/bill/sen/sb_0051-0100/scr_62_bill_20130711_introduced.pdf.

8   BlackRock, "Larry Fink's Annual Letter to CEOs: A Sense of Purpose," 2017, accessed July 18, 2018, https://www.blackrock.com/corporate/investor-relations/larry-fink-ceo-letter.

9   BlackRock, "Investment Stewardship," https://www.blackrock.com/corporate/en-us/about-us/investment-stewardship.

10   "BlackRock: Focus on Society and Profits," *New York Times,* DealBook, January 16, 2018,

https://www.nytimes.com/interactive/2018/01/16/business/dealbook/document-BlackRock-s-Laurence-Fink-Urges-C-E-O-s-to-Focus.html.

11   Sam Becker, "7 Biggest Business Blunders Ever Committed," *USA Today*, December 20, 2014, https://www.usatoday.com/story/money/business/2014/12/20/cheat-sheet-business-blunders/20627213/.

12   "Equilar Q2 2019 Gender Diversity Index," Equilar, September 11, 2019, https://www.equilar.com/reports/67-q2-2019-equilar-gender-diversity-index.html.

13   Catalyst, "Launch of Alliance for Board Diversity Calls for Fair Representation of Corporate Boards," http://www.catalyst.org/media/launch-alliance-board-diversity-calls-fair-representation-corporate-boards.

14   Thomas Gilovich and Kenneth Savitsky, "Like Goes with Like: The Role of Representativeness in Erroneous Pseudo-Scientific Beliefs," ResearchGate, January 2002, https://www.researchgate.net/publication/288842297_Like_goes_with_like_The_role_of_representativeness_in_erroneous_and_pseudo-scientific_beliefs.

15   "2016 Board Practices Report," Deloitte, accessed March 30, 2021, https://www2.deloitte.com/content/dam/Deloitte/us/Documents/center-for-board-effectiveness/us-cbe-2016-board-practices-report-a-transparent-look-at-the-work-of-the-board.pdf.

16   All Catalyst data come from "The Bottom Line: Corporate Performance and Women's Representation on Boards," 2007, http://www.catalyst.org/knowledge/bottom-line-corporate-performance-and-womens-representation-boards.

17 All citations in this paragraph come from Toyah Miller and Maria del Carmen Triana, "Demographic Diversity in the Boardroom: Mediators of the Board Diversity-Firm Performance Relationship," *Journal of Management Studies* 46, no. 5 (July 2009): 755–756, http://www.mtriana.com/mary/papers/Miller_Triana_2009.pdf.

18 "Ralph Whitworth: An Active Investor Speaks out," *This Week in the Boardroom*, July 19, 2012, https://www.youtube.com/watch?v=nqUZsKRsUT4.

19 Wikipedia, "Walt Kelly, creator of 'Pogo' comic strip," https://en.wikipedia.org/wiki/Pogo_(comic_strip)#"We_have_met_the_enemy_and_he_is_us."

20 "Russell 3000 Surpasses Milestone Marker of 20% Female Representation on Boards," Equilar, September 11, 2019, https://www.equilar.com/press-releases/115-russell-3000-surpass-milestone-marker.html.

21 Linda Landers, "Women's Purchasing Power," accessed March 30, 2021, https://girlpowermarketing.com/womens-purchasing-power/.

22 Suzanne Kahn, "Women with Access to Higher Education Changed America—But Now They're Bearing the Brunt of the Student Debt Crisis," Time, March 6, 2020, https://time.com/5797922/women-higher-education-history/.

23 Linda Landers, "Women's Purchasing Power."

24 "Corporate Fact Sheet," Discovery, accessed March 30, 2021, https://corporate.discovery.com/wp-content/uploads/2020/01/CORPORATE-FACT-SHEET_2020.pdf.

25 "Deloitte Global's latest Women in the Boardroom report highlights slow progress for gender diversity," Deloitte, October 31, 2019, https://www2.deloitte.com/id/en/pages/risk/articles/women-in-the-boardroom-report-highlights-slow-progress-for-gender-diversity-pr.html.

26 Claire Cain Miller, "Curtain Is Rising on a Tech Premiere with (As Usual) a Mostly Male Cast," *New York Times*, October 4, 2013, https://www.nytimes.com/2013/10/05/technology/as-tech-start-ups-surge-ahead-women-seem-to-be-left-behind.html.

27 Claire Cain Miller, "Twitter C.E.O. Defends Representation of Women at the Company—Sort of," *New York Times*, October 6, 2013, https://bits.blogs. nytimes.com/2013/10/06/twitter-c-e-o-defends-representation-of-women-at-the-company-sort-of/. Carrot Top is a stand-up comedian.

28 Ryan Tate, "Twitter Names Marjorie Scardino Its First Female Board Member," *Wired*, December 5, 2013, https://www.wired.com/2013/12/ twitter-board-bumbled-gender-issues/.

29 Wikipedia, "Marjorie Morris Scardino," accessed July 12, 2018, https:// en.wikipedia.org/wiki/Marjorie_Scardino.

30 Walmart, "Executive Management," https://corporate.walmart.com/our-story/ leadership.

31 "McDonald's Corp. Company Profile & Executives," *Wall Street Journal*, http://quotes.wsj.com/MCD/company-people.

32 CVS Health Investors, "Board of Directors," http://investors.cvshealth.com/ corporate-governance/board-of-directors.

33 All BlackRock quotes are from "Larry Fink's 2018 Annual Letter to CEOs," https://www.blackrock.com/corporate/investor-relations/larry-fink-ceo-letter.

34 "Buying Power: Quick Take," April 27, 2020, https://www.catalyst.org/ research/buying-power/#footnote4_q9ulgsb.

35 Jin-hui Luo, Yuangao Xiang, and Zeyue Huang, "Female Directors and Real Activities Manipulation: Evidence From China," *China Journal of Accounting Research* 10, no. 2 (June 2017): 141–166, https://www.sciencedirect.com/ science/article/pii/S1755309117300011.

36 Rihab Guider and Younes Boujelbene, "R&D-Based Earnings Management and Accounting Performance Motivation," *International Journal of Academic Research in Accounting, Finance and Management Sciences* 4, no. 2 (April 2014): 81–93, http://hrmars.com/hrmars_papers/Article_09_RD_Based_Earnings_ Management_and_Accounting1.pdf.

37 Luo, Xiang, and Huang, "Female Directors."

38   Sophie Grene and Chris Newlands, "Boards without Women Breed Scandal," *Financial Times*, March 8, 2015, https://www.ft.com/content/cdb790f8-c33d-11e4-ac3d-00144feab7de.

39   Ibid.

40   Lex Borghans, et al., "Gender Differences in Risk Aversion and Ambiguity Aversion," National Bureau of Economic Research, https://www.nber.org/system/files/working_papers/w14713/w14713.pdf.

41   "Boards without women breed scandal," *Financial Times*, accessed March 30, 2021, https://www.ft.com/content/cdb790f8-c33d-11e4-ac3d-00144feab7de.

42   Interview with Patrice Merrin, February 13, 2018.

43   "We Need Women on Boards for Many Reasons: Ethics Isn't One," The Conversation, http://theconversation.com/we-need-women-on-boards-for-many-reasons-ethics-isnt-one-37472.

44   Robert G. Eccles, "Why an Activist Hedge Fund Cares Whether Apple's Devices Are Bad for Kids," *Harvard Business Review*, January 16, 2018, https://hbr.org/2018/01/why-an-activist-hedge-fund-cares-whether-apples-devices-are-bad-for-kids.

45   "A Letter from Two Big Apple Investors Powerfully Summarizes How Smartphones Mess with Kids' Brains," Quartz, January 8, 2018, https://qz.com/1174317/a-letter-from-apple-aapl-investors-jana-partners-and-calstrs-powerfully-summarizes-how-smartphones-mess-with-kids-brains/.

46   "A Letter from Two Big Apple Investors."

47   Tony Fadell, Twitter, January 8, 2018, https://twitter.com/tfadell/status/950329842196721664.

48   Robert G. Eccles, "Why an Activist Hedge Fund Cares Whether Apple's Devices Are Bad for Kids," *Harvard Business Review*, January 16, 2018, https://hbr.org/2018/01/why-an-activist-hedge-fund-cares-whether-apples-devices-are-bad-for-kids.

49   Eccles, "Why an Activist Hedge Fund Cares."

50   Carol Hymowitz, et al., "Icahn, Loeb and Other Activists Overlook Women for Board Seats," Bloomberg, March 8, 2016, https://www. bloomberg.com/news/articles/2016-03-08/activists-from-icahn-to-loeb-overlook-women-for-board-positions.

51   Serge Moscovici and Marisa Zavalloni, "The Group As Polarizer of Attitudes," *Journal of Personality and Social Psychology* 12, no. 2 (June 1969): 125–135, https://www.researchgate.net/profile/Serge_Moscovici/ publication/232574296_The_Group_as_Polarizer_of_Attitudes/ links/542bd1080cf27e39fa91a5c2/The-Group-as-Polarizer-of-Attitudes.pdf.

52   Lynn Enright, "Why Don't Women Speak Up in Boardrooms?" The Pool, October 30, 2015, https://www.the-pool.com/work/work-news/2015/43/ why-don-t-women-speak-up-in-boardrooms.

53   Saul McLeod, "Asch Experiment," *Simply Psychology*, accessed March 21, 2018, https://www.simplypsychology.org/asch-conformity.html.

54   Mariateresa Torchia, Andrea Calabro, and Morten Huse, "Women Directors on Corporate Boards: From Tokenism to Critical Mass," *Journal of Business Ethics* 102, no. 2 (August 2011): 299–317, https://link.springer.com/ article/10.1007/s10551-011-0815-z.

55   California Senate Concurrent Resolution No. 62, https://leginfo.legislature. ca.gov/faces/billTextClient.xhtml?bill_id=201320140SCR62.

56   "Jackson to Hold Hearing Tomorrow on Women on Corporate Boards," website of State Senator Hannah-Beth Jackson, August 28, 2017, http://sd19.senate.ca.gov/ news/2017-08-28-jackson-hold-hearing-tomorrow-women-corporate-boards.

57   Torchia, Calabro, and Huse, "Women Directors."

58   Elizabeth J. McClean, Sean R. Martin, Kyle J. Emich, and Todd Woodruff, "The Social Consequences of Voice: An Examination of Voice Type and Gender on Status and Subsequent Leader Emergence," *Academy of Management Journal*, September 14, 2017, https://journals.aom.org/doi/10.5465/ amj.2016.0148.

59   Boris Groysberg and Deborah Bell, "Dysfunction in the Boardroom," *Harvard Business Review*, June 2013, https://hbr.org/2013/06/dysfunction-in-the-boardroom.

60   Interview with anonymous board member, February 2018.

61   "Companies with More Women Board Directors Experience Higher Financial Performance, According to Latest Catalyst Bottom Line Report," Catalyst, October 15, 2007, http://www.catalyst.org/media/companies-more-women-board-directors-experience-higher-financial-performance-according-latest.

62   Marcus Noland, Tyler Moran, Barbara Kotschwar, "Is Gender Diversity Profitable? Evidence from a Global Survey," Petersen Institute for International Economics, February 2016, https://www.piie.com/publications/wp/wp16-3.pdf.

63   "The Female Leadership Crisis: Why Women Are Leaving (and What We Can Do about It)," Network of Executive Women, Accenture, and Mercer, 2018, https://www.newonline.org/sites/default/files/files/NEW_Leadership_Crisis_Digitalv3.pdf.

64   Torchia, Calabro, and Huse, "Women Directors."

65   Remus Valsan, "Gender Diversity in the Boards of Directors: A Corporate Governance Perspective" (paper delivered at The European Union Centre of Excellence and University of Alberta, Edmonton, 2015).

66   Erica Hersh, "Why Diversity Matters: Women on Boards of Directors," Harvard T.H. Chan School of Public Health, July 21, 2016, https://www.hsph.harvard.edu/ecpe/why-diversity-matters-women-on-boards-of-directors/.

67   Yilmaz Arguden, "Why Boards Need More Women," *Harvard Business Review*, June 7, 2012, https://hbr.org/2012/06/why-boards-need-more-women.

68   Francesca Lagerberg, "Women in Business: The Value of Diversity," Grant Thornton International Ltd., 2015, https://www.grantthornton.global/globalassets/wib_value_of_diversity.pdf.

69   Katherine W. Phillips, Katie A. Liljenquist, and Margaret A. Neale, "Better Decisions Through Diversity, Kellogg Insight," October 1, 2010, https://insight.kellogg.northwestern.edu/article/better_decisions_through_diversity.

70   Phillips, Liljenquist, and Neale, "Better Decisions."

71   Katie Liljenquist, Katherine W. Phillips, and Margaret A. Neale, "The Pain Is Worth the Gain: The Advantages and Liabilities of Agreeing with Socially Distinct Newcomers" (presented at 16th Annual IACM Conference Melbourne, Australia, 2003), http://citeseerx.ist.psu.edu/viewdoc/download?doi=10.1.1.320.967&rep=rep1&type=pdf.

72   Wikipedia, "Vernon Jordan," accessed July 25, 2018, https://en.wikipedia.org/wiki/Vernon_Jordan.

73   Brett D. Fromson, "Jordan's 10 Board Positions Worth $1.1 Million," Washington Post, February 6, 1998, https://www.washingtonpost.com/wp-srv/politics/special/clinton/stories/director020698.htm.

74   Ebony, October 1987.

75   Black Demographics, accessed April 17, 2018, http://blackdemographics.com/.

76   Derek T. Dingle, "Power in the Boardroom: Blacks in Corporate Governance," Black Enterprise, October 9, 2019, https://www.blackenterprise.com/power-in-the-boardroom-corporate-governance/.

77   Kirwan Institute for the Study of Race and Ethnicity, accessed March 30, 2021, http://kirwaninstitute.osu.edu/.

78   Jessica Nordell, "Is This How Discrimination Ends?" Atlantic, May 7, 2017, https://www.theatlantic.com/science/archive/2017/05/unconscious-bias-training/525405/.

79   Nordell, "Is This How."

80   Wikipedia, "Rooney Rule," accessed May 1, 2018, https://en.wikipedia.org/wiki/Rooney_Rule.

81   Stefanie K. Johnson, "What Amazon's Board Was Getting Wrong about Diversity and Hiring," *Harvard Business Review*, May 14, 2018, https://hbr.org/2018/05/what-amazons-board-is-getting-wrong-about-diversity-and-hiring.

82   Martin Lipton and Jay W. Lorsch, "A Modest Proposal for Improved Corporate Governance," *Business Lawyer* 48, no. 1 (November 1992): 59–77, http://www.jstor.org/stable/40687360?read-now=1&loggedin=true&seq=6#page_scan_tab_contents.

83   Lipton and Lorsh, "A Modest Proposal."

84   "Summary of the proxy voting policy for US portfolio companies," Vanguard, accessed March 30, 2021, https://about.vanguard.com/investment-steward-ship/portfolio-company-resources/2020_proxy_voting_summary.pdf.

85   "BlackRock Investment Stewardship: Proxy voting guidelines for Us Securities," accessed March 30, 2021, BlackRock, https://www.blackrock.com/corporate/literature/fact-sheet/blk-responsible-investment-guidelines-us.pdf.

86   "Being Black in Corporate America," COQUAL, accessed March 31, 2021, https://www.talentinnovation.org/_private/assets/BeingBlack-KeyFindings-CTI.pdf.

87   Kathy Gurchiek, "6 Steps for Building an Inclusive Workplace," SHRM, March 19, 2018, https://www.shrm.org/hr-today/news/hr-magazine/0418/pages/6-steps-for-building-an-inclusive-workplace.aspx.

88   Gustavo Lopez, Neil Ruiz, and Eileen Patten, "Key facts about Asian Americans, a diverse and growing population," Pew Research Center, September 8, 2017, https://www.pewresearch.org/fact-tank/2017/09/08/key-facts-about-asian-americans/.

89   Mary Frauenfelder, "Asian-Owned Businesses Nearing Two Million," United States Census Bureau, July 27, 2016, https://www.census.gov/newsroom/blogs/random-samplings/2016/07/asian-owned-businesses-nearing-two-million.html.

90   "Asian Americans Are Expanding Their Footprint in the U.S. and Making an Impact," Nielsen, May 19, 2016, http://www.nielsen.com/us/en/insights/news/2016/Asian Americans-are-expanding-their-footprint-and-making-an-impact.html.

91   Gustavo Lopez, et al., "Key facts about Asian Americans, a diverse and growing population."

92   Grace Meng, "Corporate American's Bamboo Ceiling," The Hill, July 18, 2016, http://thehill.com/blogs/congress-blog/economy-budget/288081-corporate-americas-bamboo-ceiling.

93   "Missing Pieces Report: The 2019 Board Diversity Census of Women and Minorities on Fortune 500 Boards," Deloitte, accessed March 31, 2021, https://www2.deloitte.com/content/dam/Deloitte/us/Documents/center-for-board-effectiveness/us-cbe-missing-pieces-report-2018-board-diversity-census.pdf.

94   Ellen McGirt, "raceAhead: The Asian Glass Ceiling," Fortune, June 4, 2018, https://fortune.com/2018/06/04/raceahead-asian-glass-ceiling/.

95   Victoria Namkung, "The model minority myth says all Asians are successful. Why that's dangerous," NBC News, March 20, 2021, https://www.nbcnews.com/news/asian-america/model-minority-myth-says-asians-are-successful-dangerous-rcna420.

96   Meng, "Corporate America's Bamboo Ceiling."

97   Karthick Ramakrishnan and Jennifer Lee, "Op-Ed: Despite what you might have heard, Asian American CEOs are the exception, not the norm," Los Angeles Times, October 19, 2017, https://www.latimes.com/opinion/op-ed/la-oe-ramakrishnan-lee-asian-american-executives-20171019-story.html.

98   "Chinese Exclusion Act (1882)," ourdocuments.gov, accessed April 26, 2018, https://www.ourdocuments.gov/doc.php?flash=false&doc=47.

99   Wikipedia, "Internment of Japanese Americans," accessed April 26, 2018, https://en.wikipedia.org/wiki/Internment_of_Japanese_Americans.

100   Wikipedia, "Internment of Japanese Americans."

101 "Asian Americans Then and Now," Center for Global Education, accessed March 31, 2021, https://asiasociety.org/education/asian-americans-then-and-now.

102 Jackson G. Lu, Richard E. Nisbett, and Michael W. Morris, "Why East Asians but no South Asians are underrepresented in leadership positions in the United States," February 18, 2020, https://www.pnas.org/content/117/9/4590.

103 Kimmy Yam, "The mental health toll of being a 'model minority' in 2020," NBC News, December 23, 2020, https://www.nbcnews.com/news/asian-america/mental-health-toll-being-model-minority-2020-n1249949.

104 Alexis Xydias, "Asian Millennials Will Rule, If They Temper Their Ambition," CNBC: Asia Tomorrow, July 17, 2015, https://www.cnbc.com/2015/07/17/are-asian-millennials-just-too-ambitious-to-become-ceo.html

105 Stefanie K. Johnson and Thomas Sy, "Why Aren't There More Asian Americans in Leadership Positions," *Harvard Business Review*, December 19, 2016, https://hbr.org/2016/12/why-arent-there-more-Asian-Americans-in-leadership-positions.

106 "Media Diversity," Asian Americans Advancing Justice, accessed March 31, 2021, https://advancingjustice-aajc.org/media-diversity.

107 "Asian Pacific Americans: in Prime Time," National Asian Pacific American Legal Consortium, accessed March 31, 2021, https://www.aapisontv.com/uploads/3/8/1/3/38136681/yuen2005.pdf.

108 "Asian Pacific American Media Coalition Issues Diversity Report Cards to TV Networks," Japanese American Citizens League, May 1, 2018, https://jacl.org/statements/asian-pacific-american-media-coalition-issues-diversity-report-cards-to-tv-networks?rq=report%20card.

109 Eva Shang, "CEOs in the Making: The Youngest Asian Americans in Tech," CBS News, February 22, 2016, https://www.nbcnews.com/news/asian-america/ceos-making-youngest-Asian Americans-tech-n516691.

110 Wikipedia, "Ellen Pao," accessed April 26, 2018, https://en.wikipedia.org/wiki/Ellen_Pao.

111 "Boardroom Accountability Project," New York City Comptroller, September 6, 2017, https://comptroller.nyc.gov/services/financial-matters/boardroom-accountability-project/boardroom-accountability-project-2-0/.

112 Scott M. Stringer, letter sent to nominating/governance committee chairs of portfolio companies held by NYC Pension Funds, September 6, 2017, https://comptroller.nyc.gov/wp-content/uploads/2017/09/BAP-2.0-Letter-A.pdf.

113 "Comptroller Stringer, NYC Funds: New Corporate Governance Guidelines for City Pension Funds Call for Greater Gender, Racial & LGBT Diversity on Corporate Boards," May 20, 2016, https://comptroller.nyc.gov/newsroom/comptroller-stringer-nyc-funds-new-corporate-governance-guidelines-for-city-pension-funds-call-for-greater-gender-racial-lgbt-diversity-on-corporate-boards/.

114 Jack Linshi, "The Real Problem When It Comes to Diversity and Asian Americans," *Time*, October 14, 2014, http://time.com/3475962/Asian American-diversity/

115 Linshi, "The Real Problem."

116 "Corporate Equality Index 2019," Human Rights Campaign Foundation, accessed March 31, 2021, https://assets2.hrc.org/files/assets/resources/CEI-2019-FullReport.pdf?_ga=2.201855633.101864699.1554205991-2015291853.1552927569.

117 Blake Ellis, "Record Number of U.S. Firms Offering Same-Sex Benefits," CNN Money, December 9, 2013, http://money.cnn.com/2013/12/09/pf/lgbt-corporate-equality/index.html.

118 "Visibility Counts: The LGBTQ+ Board Leadership Opportunity," Out Leadership, accessed March 31, 2021, https://outleadership.com/wp-content/uploads/2021/02/2.2.21-Out-Leadership-Quorum-Board-Diversity-Report.pdf?utm_source=Quorum+Report+Download&utm_campaign=a02741ffff-AUTOMATION_Welcome_Message_1&utm_medium=email&utm_

term=0_d3de37f0b1-a02741ffff-378961546&mc_cid=a02741ffff&mc_eid=63175ff5e0.

119 Patricia Lenkov, "Diversity 5.0—Diversity in the Boardroom," LinkedIn, January 5, 2016, https://www.linkedin.com/pulse/diversity-50-lgbt-boardroom-patricia-lenkov/.

120 Laura Moreno, "This Is Why the Future Will Be Queer," Metrosource, July 25, 2019, https://metrosource.com/this-is-why-the-future-will-be-queer/.

121 Lenkov, "Diversity 5.0."

122 Bill George, Peter Sims, Andrew N. McLean, and Diana Mayer, "Discovering Your Authentic Leadership," *Harvard Business Review*, February 2007, https://hbr.org/2007/02/discovering-your-authentic-leadership

123 George et al., "Discovering Your Authentic Leadership."

124 Todd Sears, email message to Patricia Lenkov, March 14, 2018.

125 Out Leadership, https://outleadership.com/.

126 "Quorum, Dedicated to Increasing Representation of Openly LGBT Directors on Corporate Boards, Launches in San Francisco," Out Leadership, October 25, 2015, https://outleadership.com/insights/quorum-dedicated-to-increasing-representation-of-openly-lgbt-directors-on-corporate-boards-launches-in-san-francisco/.

127 "Quirom: Out Leadership LGBT+ Board Diversity Guidelines," https://boardleadership.kpmg.us/content/dam/boardleadership/en/pdf/2018/out-leadership-lgbt-board-diversity-guidelines.pdf.

128 Todd Sears email.

129 Patricia Lenkov, "LGBT+ in the Boardroom," Ethical Boardroom, accessed May 7, 2018, https://ethicalboardroom.com/lgbt-in-the-boardroom/.

130 Conversation with Jim Norberg, March 1, 2018.

131 Lenkov, "Diversity 5.0."

132 "Quorum: Out Leadership's LGBT+ Board Diversity Guidelines," Out Leadership, https://outleadership.com/wp-content/uploads/2021/02/2.2.21-Out-Leadership-Quorum-Board-Diversity-Report.pdf?utm_source=Quorum+Report+Download&utm_campaign=a02741ffff-AUTOMATION_Welcome_Message_1&utm_medium=email&utm_term=0_d3de37f0b1-a02741ffff-378961546&mc_cid=a02741ffff&mc_eid=63175ff5e0.

133 Interview with Paul Wendel, February 22, 2018.

134 Interview with Paul Wendel.

135 Garance Franke-Ruta, "How America Got Past the Anti-Gay Politics of the '90s," *Atlantic*, April 8, 2013, https://www.theatlantic.com/politics/archive/2013/04/how-america-got-past-the-anti-gay-politics-of-the-90s/266976/.

136 Sara A. Harvard, "Is Same-Sex Marriage Legal in All 50 States? Despite Supreme Court Ruling, It's Complicated," Mic Network, July 5, 2016, https://mic.com/articles/147670/is-same-sex-marriage-legal-in-all-states#.bdhZ2TU85.

137 Wikipedia, "LGBT+ Adoption in the United States," accessed May 8, 2018, https://en.wikipedia.org/wiki/LGBT_adoption_in_the_United_States.

138 "Legislation affecting LGBT+ rights across the country," ACLU, accessed May 8, 2018, https://www.aclu.org/other/legislation-affecting-lgbt-rights-across-country.

139 Interview with Paul Wendel.

140 See chapter 5.

141 "Governing Board Diversity, 2014 Survey Results," California Department of Insurance, Insurance Diversity Initiative, December 8, 2014, http://www.insurance.ca.gov/diversity/05-gbd/05-2014-GBD-Survey/upload/GBD-2014-Survey-Results-FINAL-2.pdf.

142 "California Mandates Diversity Quotas for Corporate Boards," National Law Review, October 5, 2020, https://www.natlawreview.com/article/california-mandates-diversity-quotas-corporate-boards.

143 Interview with Stephanie Sandberg, February 22, 2018.

144 Interview with Stephanie Sandberg.

145 "The future is fluid: Generation Z's approach to gender and sexuality is indeed revolutionary," Daily Dot, October 18, 2017, https://www.dailydot.com/irl/generation-z-fluid/.

146 *GLAAD* blog, March 31, 2021, https://www.glaad.org/blog/new-glaad-study-reveals-twenty-percent-millennials-identify-LGBTQ+.

147 "Hispanics in the US Fast Facts," CNN, February 24, 2021, https://www.cnn.com/2013/09/20/us/hispanics-in-the-u-s-/index.html.

148 "Latino/a and Hispanic Culture in the U.S.," InterExchange, June 22, 2020, https://www.interexchange.org/articles/visit-the-usa/latino-hispanic-culture-in-us/.

149 Patricia Guadalupe, "Organization Advocates for More Latinos on Corporate Boards," NBC News, May 9, 2016, https://www.nbcnews.com/news/latino/organization-advocates-more-latinos-corporate-boards-n570476.

150 "Excluding Hispanics from the Boardroom," Houston Hispanic Chamber of Commerce, May 3, 2019, https://www.houstonhispanicchamber.com/in-the-news/2019/05/03/excluding-hispanics-from-the-boardroom/.

151 Cesar Melgoza, "Hispanics in the Boardroom: Glass Ceiling or Foggy Windshield," July 28, 2017, https://www.huffpost.com/entry/hispanics-in-the-boardroo_b_11225918.

152 "The Hispanic Potential Buying Power of 1.7 Trillion Dollars," NAWRB, February 28, 2019, https://www.nawrb.com/hispanic-buying-power/.

153 "Missing Pieces Report," Deloitte, https://www2.deloitte.com/us/en/pages/center-for-board-effectiveness/articles/missing-pieces-fortune-500-board-diversity-study-2018.html.

154 Katie Kuehner-Herbert, "More Hispanics Are Needed on Boards," Corporate Board Member, https://boardmember.com/more-hispanics-are-needed-on-boards/.

155 Victor Arias, Jr., "The Missing Pieces Latinos in the Boardroom," Latino Leaders, https://www.latinoleadersmagazine.com/summer-2019/2019/12/5/the-missing-pieces-latinos-in-the-boardroom.

156 J. D. Swerzenski, Donald Tomaskovic-Devey, and Eric Hoyt, "This Is Where There Are the Most Hispanic Executives and Its Not Where You Think," Fast Company, January 28, 2020, https://www.fastcompany.com/90456329/this-is-where-there-are-the-most-hispanic-executives-and-its-not-where-you-think.

157 Cesar Melgoza, "Hispanics in the Boardroom."

158 Katie Kuehner-Herbert, "More Hispanics Are Needed."

159 Laura Huang, Marcia Frideger, and Jone L. Pearce, "How Non-Native Speakers Can Crack the Glass Ceiling," *Harvard Business Review*, June 2014, https://hbr.org/2014/06/how-non-native-speakers-can-crack-the-glass-ceiling.

160 "The Glass Ceiling Facing Nonnative English Speakers," Knowledge@Wharton, December 17, 2013, https://knowledge.wharton.upenn.edu/article/glass-ceiling-facing-nonnative-english-speakers/.

161 Luis Noe-Bustamante, "Education levels of recent Latino immigrants in the U.S. reached new highs as of 2018," Pew Research Center: FactTank, April 7, 2020, https://www.pewresearch.org/fact-tank/2020/04/07/education-levels-of-recent-latino-immigrants-in-the-u-s-reached-new-highs-as-of-2018/.

162 Joel McFarland et al., "The Condition of Education," IES: National Center for Education Statistics, May 2017, https://nces.ed.gov/pubs2017/2017144.pdf.

163 J. D. Swerzenski, Donald Tomaskovic-Devey, and Eric Hoyt, "Where Are the Hispanic Executives?" The Conversation, January 22, 2020, http://theconversation.com/where-are-the-hispanic-executives-128981.

164 Swerzenski, Tomaskovic-Devey, and Hoyt, "Where Are the Hispanic Executives?"

165 Michael Toebe, The Risks and Realities of Overboarding, Corporate Compliance Insights, January 30,2020, https://www.corporatecomplianceinsights.com/risks-realities-overboarding/.

166 "LCDA Board Tracker," Latino Corporate Directors Association, https:// mms.latinocorporatedirectors.org/members/directory/search_board_lcda. php?org_id=LCDA.

167 Richard Fry, "Millennials are the largest generation in the U.S. labor force," Pew Research Center: Fact Tank, April 11, 2018, https://www.pewresearch. org/fact-tank/2018/04/11/millennials-largest-generation-us-labor-force/.

168 Laura Gayle, "How Generation Z Is Transforming the Workplace," FEI, August 22, 2019, https://www.financialexecutives.org/FEI-Daily/August-2019/How-Generation-Z-Is-Transforming-the-Workplace.aspx#:~:text=Research%20 and%20data%20project%20that,business%20can%20afford%20to%20ignore.

169 Amy Adkins, "Millennials: The Job-Hopping Generation," Galluphttps:// www.gallup.com/workplace/231587/millennials-job-hopping-genera-tion.aspx#:~:text=A%20recent%20Gallup%20report%20on,U.S.%20 economy%20%2430.5%20billion%20annually.

170 Meaghan Kilroy, "CtW Investment Group Calls on Amazon to Improve Gender Diversity," *Pensions & Investments*, December 6, 2017, http://www.pionline.com/article/20171206/ONLINE/171209897/ ctw-investment-group-calls-on-amazon-to-improve-gender-diversity.

171 Jason Del Rey, "Amazon Employees Are Outraged by Their Company's Opposition to a Plan to Add More Diversity to Its Board," Recode, May 8, 2018, https://www.recode.net/2018/5/8/17328466/amazon-jeff-bezos-board-diversity-proposal-shareholder-vote.

172 Wikipedia, "Rooney Rule," accessed June 7, 2018, https://en.wikipedia.org/ wiki/Rooney_Rule.

173 Cale Guthrie Weissman, "Report: Amazon Board's Diversity Stance Draws Fire from Amazon Employees," *Fast Company*, May 8, 2018, https://www. fastcompany.com/40569756/report-amazon-boards-diversity-stance-draws-fire-from-amazon-employees.

174 Del Rey, "Amazon Employees."

175 Ethan Baron, "Amazon Follows Bay Area Tech Companies on NFL 'Rooney Rule' For Diversity," *Mercury News*, May 15, 2018, https://www.mercurynews.

com/2018/05/15amazon-follows-bay-area-tech-companies-on-nfl-rooney-rule-for-diversity/.

176 Julie Sweet and Ellyn Shook, "The Hidden Value of Culture Makers," Accenture, https://www.accenture.com/us-en/about/inclusion-diversity/culture-equality-research.

177 Lilah Raptopoulos, Laura Noonan, and Sarah Gordon, "Do Company Diversity Programmes Actually Help Women Get Ahead?" *Financial Times*, accessed May 10, 2018, https://ig.ft.com/company-diversity-employee-views/.

178 Tessa L. Dover, Brenda Major, and Cheryl R. Kaiser, "Members of High-Status Groups Are Threatened by Pro-Diversity Organizational Messages," *Journal of Experimental Social Psychology* 62 (2016): 58–67, https://pdfs.semanticscholar.org/0cc0/3cb745610039bb84319cdec5fcf65aa08f1a.pdf.

179 James Damore, "Google's Ideological Echo Chamber," July 2017, https://assets.documentcloud.org/documents/3914586/Googles-Ideological-Echo-Chamber.pdf.

180 Daisuke Wakabayashi, "Contentious Memo Strikes Nerve Inside Google and Out," *New York Times*, August 8, 2017, https://www.nytimes.com/2017/08/08/technology/google-engineer-fired-gender-memo.html.

181 Amit Batish, "Russell 3000 Boards On Pace to Achieve Gender Parity by 2034," Harvard Law School Forum on Corporate Governance and Financial Regulation, April 5, 2019, https://corpgov.law.harvard.edu/2019/04/05/russell-3000-boards-on-pace-to-achieve-gender-parity-by-2034/, accessed May 19, 2019.

182 Susan Fowler, "Reflecting on One Very, Very Strange Year at Uber," personal blog, February 19, 2017, https://www.susanjfowler.com/blog/2017/2/19/reflecting-on-one-very-strange-year-at-uber.

183 Salvador Rodriguez, "Uber Versus Women: A Timeline," *Inc.*, March 28, 2017, https://www.inc.com/salvador-rodriguez/uber-women-timeline.html.

184 Khadeja Safdar, "Victoria's Secret Boss Bets on a Radical Idea: Smartphones Will Fade," *Wall Street Journal*, February 5, 2018, https://www.wsj.com/

articles/the-boss-of-victorias-secret-bets-on-a-radical-idea-smartphones-will-fade-1517849668.

185 Richard Nieva, "At Shareholder Meeting, Google's Diversity Issues Take Center Stage," CNET, June 6, 2018, https://www.cnet.com/news/at-alphabet-shareholder-meeting-google-diversity-issues-take-center-stage/.

186 Christina Binkley, "Dolce & Gabbana's Quest for Youth," *Wall Street Journal*, May 16, 2018, https://www.wsj.com/articles/dolce-gabbanas-quest-for-youth-1526652257.

187 Joshua Glass, "Tour Dolce & Gabbana's New Clubhouse for Millennials in Soho," *New York Post*, April 11, 2018, https://nypost.com/2018/04/11/tour-dolce-gabbanas-new-clubhouse-for-millennials-in-soho/.

188 Glass, "Tour Dolce."

189 Sarah Butler, "Burberry's Sales Growth Slows Despite 'Exceptional' UK Performance," *Guardian*, April 21, 2017, https://www.theguardian.com/business/2017/apr/19/slump-in-burberry-shares-as-global-sales-growth-slows.

190 Glass, "Tour Dolce."

191 "Retirement Age," Wikipedia, https://en.wikipedia.org/wiki/Retirement_age.

192 "L Brands Inc.," *Wall Street Journal*, accessed May 27, 2018, https://quotes.wsj.com/LB/company-people.

193 "Age Diversity within Boards of Directors of the S&P Companies," KPMG, March 30, 2017, https://home.kpmg.com/jm/en/home/insights/2017/03/age-diversity-within-boards-of-directors-of-the-s-p-500-companie.html.

194 Oliver Staley, "The Type of Diversity Boardrooms Prize Most Is Age—and They Can't Even Manage That," Quartz at Work, April 25, 2018, https://work.qz.com/1260792/the-type-of-diversity-boardrooms-prize-most-is-age-and-they-cant-even-manage-that/.

195 Ibid.

196 Brad Power, "3 Ways Big Companies Are Connecting with Younger Consumers," *Harvard Business Review*, October 26, 2015, https://hbr.org/2015/10/three-ways-big-companies-are-connecting-with-younger-consumers.

197 Power, "3 Ways."

198 Joshua Kim, "Technology Since 1998," Inside Higher Ed, January 6, 2014, https://www.insidehighered.com/blogs/technology-and-learning/technology-1998.

199 Wikipedia, "Instagram," accessed May 27, 2018, https://en.wikipedia.org/wiki/Instagram.

200 Wikipedia, "Pinterest," accessed May 27, 2018, https://en.wikipedia.org/wiki/Pinterest.

201 Anthony Goodman, "How Old Is Too Old?" *Financial Times*, November 2, 2010, https://www.ft.com/content/5b0ce702-e5bf-11df-b023-00144feabdc0.

202 Annie Gasparro and Jacob Bunge, "Food Companies Churn through CEOs, Desperate for Fresh Ideas," *Wall Street Journal*, May 29, 2018, https://www.wsj.com/articles/packaged-food-companies-churn-through-ceos-desperate-for-fresh-ideas-1527598800.

203 Ibid.

204 Ibid.

205 Power, "3 Ways."

206 Jacqueline Muna Musiitwa, "Companies Need More Millennial Board Members If They Want to Stay Relevant," Quartz at Work, April 23, 2015, https://qz.com/389387/companies-need-more-millennial-board-members-if-they-want-to-stay-relevant/.

207 John C. Maxwell, *Good Leaders Ask Great Questions: Your Foundation for Successful Leadership* (New York: Center Street | Hachette Book Group, 2014).

208 Sid Saraf, "That's How It's Done: Athletes Who Went out on Top," Fox Sports, October 20, 2016, https://www.foxsports.com/buzzer/gallery/nfl-nba-mlb-michael-jordan-michael-strahan-athletes-who-went-out-on-top-041615.

209 Ibid.

210 Wikipedia, "David Robinson (basketball)," accessed May 29, 2018, https://en.wikipedia.org/wiki/David_Robinson_(basketball).

211 Wikipedia, "Ned Jarrett," accessed May 29, 2018, https://en.wikipedia.org/wiki/Ned_Jarrett.

212 Wikipedia, "Joe DiMaggio," accessed May 29, 2018, https://en.wikipedia.org/wiki/Joe_DiMaggio.

213 Wikipedia, "Rocky Marciano," accessed May 29, 2018, https://en.wikipedia.org/wiki/Rocky_Marciano.

214 Ronald Masulis, Cong Wang, Fei Xie, and Shuram Zhang, "Older and Wiser, or Too Old to Govern?" paper presented at the 2016 American Economic Association, December 31, 2016, http://www.cicfconf.org/sites/default/files/paper_703.pdf.

215 Wikipedia, "Numerus Clausus," accessed May 16, 2018, https://en.wikipedia.org/wiki/Numerus_clausus#United_States.

216 Kalefa Sanneh, "The Limits of 'Diversity,'" *New Yorker*, October 9, 2017, https://www.newyorker.com/magazine/2017/10/09/the-limits-of-diversity.

217 Associated Press, "Asian American Groups File Racial Quotas Complaint against Harvard University," *Guardian*, May 16, 2015, https://www.theguardian.com/education/2015/may/16/Asian American-groups-file-racial-quotas-complaint-against-harvard-university.

218 Wikipedia, "The Immigration Act of 1924," accessed May 16, 2018, https://en.wikipedia.org/wiki/Immigration_Act_of_1924.

219 Kristen Carroll, "Norway's Companies Act: A 10-Year Look at Gender Equality, " *Pace International Law Review* 26, no. 1 (Spring 2014), https://digitalcommons.pace.edu/cgi/viewcontent.cgi?article=1338&context=pilr.

220 Remus Valsan, "Gender Diversity in the Boards of Directors: A Corporate Governance Perspective" (working paper, University of Edinburgh, School of

Law, November 2, 2015), https://cloudfront.ualberta.ca/-/media/eucentre/pdfs/working-papers/remus-valsanworking-papergender-diversity.pdf).

221 Ibid.

222 Ibid.

223 Julia Boorstin, "At the current rate, corporate boards won't hit gender parity until 2032, new report warns," CNBC, March 5, 2021, https://www.cnbc.com/2021/03/05/corporate-boards-wont-hit-gender-parity-until-2032-new-report-warns.html.

224 "Rekindle 'M Factor' in Every Woman," Boardroom Diversity, June 2, 2013, http://www.boardroomdiversity.org/rekindle-m-factor-in-every-woman/.

225 "The Spread of Gender Quotas for Company Boards," *Economist*, March 25, 2014, https://www.economist.com/the-economist-explains/2014/03/25/the-spread-of-gender-quotas-for-company-boards.

226 Neeka Choobineh, "Gender Quotas for Corporate Boards: A Holistic Analysis" (University of Pennsylvania, Joseph Wharton Scholars, May 2, 2016), https://repository.upenn.edu/cgi/viewcontent.cgi?article=1004&context=joseph_wharton_scholars.

227 Valsan, "Gender Diversity."

228 Valsan, "Gender Diversity."

229 Julie-Anne Sprague and Joanna Mather, "ASX Writes 30pc Gender Target into Governance Guidelines," *Australian Financial Review*, May 2, 2018, https://www.afr.com/business/asx-writes-30pc-gender-target-into-governance-guidelines-20180502-h0zite.

230 Valsan, "Gender Diversity."

231 Valsan, "Gender Diversity."

232 Valsan, "Gender Diversity."

233 Valsan, "Gender Diversity." The Davies Review included the threat of mandatory quotas being imposed by the EU, but under the terms of Brexit, it is unclear whether the threat still holds.

234 "One of five of UK's top FSE 350 firms warned over gender diversity," BBC, February 2020, https://www.bbc.com/news/business-51685731.

235 Cydney Posner, "A First Challenge to California's Board Diversity Law," Harvard Law School Forum on Corporate Governance, September 4, 2019, https://corpgov.law.harvard.edu/2019/09/04/a-first-challenge-to-californias-board-gender-diversity-law/.

236 *H.J.R. 17-1017, 2017 Gen. Assemb., Reg. Sess. (Colo. 2017); S.R. 1007, 189th Gen. Court, Reg. Sess. (Mass. 2015); H.R. 273, 2017 Gen. Assemb., Reg. Sess. (Pa. 2017).*

237 The Alliance for Board Diversity consists of four leadership organizations: Catalyst, the Executive Leadership Council, the Hispanic Association on Corporate Responsibility, and Leadership for Asian Pacific's. See Deloitte, "Missing Pieces Report: The 2016 Board Diversity Census of Women and Minorities on Fortune 500 Boards," February 6, 2017, https://www2.deloitte.com/content/dam/Deloitte/us/Documents/center-for-corporate-governance/us-board-diversity-census-missing-pieces.pdf.

238 Deloitte, "Missing Pieces Report."

239 Valsan, "Gender Diversity."

240 Aimee Picchi, "For higher profits, add women at the top," CBS News, September 26, 2016, https://www.cbsnews.com/news/for-higher-profits-add-women-at-the-top/, accessed May 19, 2019.

241 Deloitte, "Missing Pieces Report."

242 Deloitte, "Missing Pieces Report."

243 "SB-826 Corporations: boards of directors," California Legislative Information, October 1, 2018, https://leginfo.legislature.ca.gov/faces/billTextClient.xhtml?bill_id=201720180SB826. Accessed May 14, 2019.

244 Michael D. Kane, "Massachusetts' Legislature Wants More Women on Boards of Directors," MassLive, https://www.masslive.com/news/worcester/index.ssf/2015/10/massachusetts_legislature_want.html.

245 Julie Carriew, "We Can't Just Ask Politely:" California's Push for Gender Quotas on Company Boards," Guardian, July 4, 2018, https://www.theguardian.com/us-news/2018/jul/04/california-gender-quotas-company-boards

246 Joann S. Lublin, "New York State Fund Snubs All-Male Boards," *Wall Street Journal*, March 20, 2018, https://www.wsj.com/articles/new-york-state-fund-snubs-all-male-boards-1521538321.

247 Sarah Krouse, "BlackRock: Companies Should Hire at Least Two Female Directors," *Wall Street Journal*, February 2, 2018, https://www.wsj.com/articles/blackrock-companies-should-have-at-least-two-female-directors-1517598407.

248 Danielle Wiener-Bronner, "'Fearless Girl' Is Moving to a New Home," CNN Money, April 19, 2018, http://money.cnn.com/2018/04/19/news/companies/fearless-girl-moving-nyse/index.html.

249 Business Roundtable, accessed June 20, 2018, https://www.businessroundtable.org/.

250 Business Roundtable, "Principles of Corporate Governance," 2016, accessed June 20, 2018, https://businessroundtable.org/sites/default/files/Principles-of-Corporate-Governance-2016.pdf.

251 Business Roundtable, "Members," accessed June 20, 2018, https://www.businessroundtable.org/about/members.

252 Business Roundtable, "Principles of Corporate Governance."

253 General Motors, "Board of Directors," accessed June 20, 2018, https://www.gm.com/company/leadership/board-of-directors.html.

254 Governance Principles, "Commonsense Corporate Governance Principles," accessed June 20, 2018, http://www.governanceprinciples.org/.

255 Ibid.

256 Interview with Beverly Neufeld, May 23, 2018.

257 "Report on the Status of New York Women and Girls, 2018 Outlook," New York State Council on Women and Girls, 2018, accessed June 20, 2018, https://www.ny.gov/sites/ny.gov/files/atoms/files/StatusNYWomenGirls2018Outlook.pdf.

258 MeToo, accessed June 20, 2018, https://metoomvmt.org/.

259 Interview with Beverly Neufeld.

260 Helen Raleigh, "Evidence from Norway Shows Gender Quotas Don't Work for Women," *Federalist*, March 13, 2018, http://thefederalist.com/2018/03/13/evidence-from-norway-shows-gender-quotas-dont-work-for-women/.

261 "Revealed: The worst explanations for not appointing women to FTSE company boards," GOV.UK, https://www.gov.uk/government/news/revealed-the-worst-explanations-for-not-appointing-women-to-ftse-company-boards.

262 Emma Hinchliffe, "The number of female CEOs in the Fortune 500 hits an all-time record," *Fortune*, May 18, 2020, https://fortune.com/2020/05/18/women-ceos-fortune-500-2020/.

263 "Women in Management: Quick Take," Catalyst, August 11, 2020, https://www.catalyst.org/research/women-in-management/.

264 Phil Wahba, "The number of black CEOs in Fortune 500 remains very low," June 1, 2020, https://fortune.com/2020/06/01/black-ceos-fortune-500-2020-african-american-business-leaders/.

265 "Only 9 Hispanic CEOs at top 500 companies," September 10, 2020. https://mexican-american-proarchive.com/2020/09/only-9-hispanic-ceos-at-top-500-companies/.

266 "MIT Study Explains Why American Business Leaders Are More Likely to Be Indian Than Chinese," February 20, 2020, https://www.marketwatch.com/story/mit-study-explains-why-american-business-leaders-are-more-likely-to-be-indian-than-chinese-2020-02-20.

267 Tanya Dua, "The Most Innovative Chief Marketing Officers of 2020," Business Insider, July 7, 2020, https://www.businessinsider.com/the-most-innovative-chief-marketing-officers-of-2020-6.

268 "Hirable Like Me," Kellogg Insight, April 3, 2013, https://insight.kellogg. northwestern.edu/article/hirable_like_me.

269 "PWC's 2020 Annual Corporate Directors Survey: Turning crisis into opportunity," PWC, https://www.pwc.com/us/en/services/governance-insights-center/ assets/pwc-2020-annual-corporate-directors-survey.pdf.

270 Kendra Cherry, "What Is Cognitive Bias? VeryWellMind, July 19, 2020, https://www.verywellmind.com/what-is-a-cognitive-bias-2794963.

271 David F. Larcker and Brian Tayan, "Seven Myths of Boards of Directors," Stanford Business, October 12, 2015, https://www.gsb.stanford.edu/insights/ seven-myths-boards-directors.

272 Claire Hillman, "The Fortune 500 Has More Female CEOs Than Ever Before," Fortune, May 16, 2016, https://fortune.com/2019/05/16/ fortune-500-female-ceos/.

273 Wahba, "The number of black CEOs."

274 "Only 9 Hispanic CEOs at Top 500 Companies."

275 "Gartner Says 69% of Boards of Directors Accelerated Their Digital Business Initiatives Following COVID-19 Disruptions," Gartner, September 30, 2020, https://www.gartner.com/en/newsroom/press-releases/2020-09-30-gartner- says-sixty-nine-percent-of-boards-of-directors-accelerated-their-digital-busi- ness-initiatives-folloing-covid-19-disruptions.

276 Steven Foley, Jennifer Bissell, and David Oakley, "US board composition: male, stale and frail?" *Financial Times*, August 15, 2016, https://ig.ft.com/ sites/us-board-diversity/.

277 "Board Refreshment Trends at S&P 1500 Firms," ISS Insights, https://www. issgovernance.com/board-refreshment-trends-sp-1500-firms/.

278 Ning Jia, "Should Directors Have Term Limits? Evidence from Corporate Innovation," *European Accounting Review* 26, no. 4, June 2016, https://www. researchgate.net/publication/304401312_Should_Directors_Have_Term_ Limits_-_Evidence_from_Corporate_Innovation.

279 Davis Polk Governance Briefing.

280 Ibid.

281 "Board composition: The road to strategic refreshment and succession," PWC, https://www.pwc.com/us/en/governance-insights-center/publications/assets/ pwc-board-composition-the-road-to-strategic-refreshment-and-succession.pdf

282 Ken Wilcox, "Culture Trumps Strategy," Stanford eCorner, March 5, 2008, https://ecorner.stanford.edu/wp-content/uploads/sites/2/2008/03/1965.pdf.

283 "6 Steps for Building an Inclusive Workplace," SHRM, March 19, 2018, https://www.shrm.org/hr-today/news/hr-magazine/0418/pages/6-steps-for-building-an-inclusive-workplace.aspx

284 "Early Childhood Education," National Education Association, https:// www.nea.org/student-success/smart-just-policies/funding-public-schools/ early-childhood-education.

285 Elizabeth A. Shuey and Miloš Kankaraš "The Power and Promise of Early Learning," OECD iLibrary, November 7, 2018, https://www.oecd-ilibrary. org/docserver/f9b2e53f-en.pdf?expires=1607281636&id=id&accname=gue st&checksum=09B6BE97B390C25F74516F6FD5C429FB.

286 "Public High School Graduation Rates," IES: National Center for Education Statistics, May 2020, https://nces.ed.gov/programs/coe/indicator_coi.asp.

287 Cristobal de Bray et al., "Status and Trends in the Education of Racial and Ethnic Groups 2018," IES: National Center for Education Statistics, https:// nces.ed.gov/pubs2019/2019038.pdf.

288 de Bray, "Status and Trends."

289 The Centre For Global Inclusion, https://centreforglobalinclusion.org/about/.

290 Karen Brown, "To Retain Employees, Focus on Inclusion, Not Just Diversity," Harvard Business Review, December 4, 2018, https://hbr.org/2018/12/ to-retain-employees-focus-on-inclusion-not-just-diversity.

291 "The 2017 Tech Leavers Report," Kapor Center, https://www.kaporcenter.org/ tech-leavers/.

292 Matteo Tonello, "Corporate Board Practices," Esgauge: Conference Board, https://conferenceboard.esgauge.org/boardpractices.

293 Wikipedia, "The Rooney Rule."

294 Wikipedia, "The Rooney Rule."

295 Willis Towers Watson, "Compensation for outside corporate directors increased 3% to over $267,000 in 2017, Willis Towers Watson study finds," September 6, 2018, accessed May 13, 2019, https://www.willistowerswatson.com/en/press/2018/09/compensation-for-outside-corporate-directors-increased 3-percent-in-2017.